The Big Book of Halloween

The Big Book of Halloween

Creative & Creepy Projects for Revellers of All Ages

by
Laura Dover Doran

LARK
BOOKS

ASHEVILLE, NORTH CAROLINA

BOOK AND COVER DESIGN:
Chris Bryant

PHOTOGRAPHY:
Evan Bracken

ILLUSTRATIONS:
(FOR PROJECTS) Don Osby
(FOR GHOST STORIES) Jean Wall Penland

EDITORIAL ASSISTANCE:
Heather Smith, Catharine Sutherland,
and Evans Carter

PRODUCTION ASSISTANCE:
Hannes Charen and Val Anderson

Library of Congress Cataloging-in-Publication Data

Doran, Laura Dover, 1970–
    The big book of Halloween : creative & creepy projects for
revellers of all ages / by Laura Dover Doran.—1st. ed.
        p.   cm.
    Includes index.
    ISBN 1-57990-063-1
    1. Halloween decorations.   I. Title
TT900.H32D67   1998
745.5941—dc21   98–16054
                                                              CIP

10 9 8 7 6 5 4 3

Published by Lark Books
50 College St.
Asheville, NC 28801, USA

© 1998, Lark Books

For information about distribution in the U.S., Canada, the U.K., Europe,
and Asia, call Lark Books at 828-253-0467.

Distributed in Australia by Capricorn Link (Australia) Pty Ltd., P.O. Box
6651, Baulkham Hills Business Centre, NSW 2153, Australia

Distributed in New Zealand by Southern Publishers Group, 22
Burleigh St., Grafton, Auckland, NZ

Printed in Hong Kong

ISBN 1-57990-063-1

For Austin,
born Halloween 1997

Contents

Acknowledgments

Special thanks to the following people who provided information, props, or otherwise assisted me in preparing this book: Ivo Ballentine, Pam Beattie, Cathy Blankenship, Hattie Burgin, Brian Caskey, Patrick Doran, Scott Gerken, Kathy Holmes, Dana Irwin, Katherine Kaderabek, Todd Kaderabek, Mardi Letson, Deborah Morgenthal, Jean Wall Penland, Bud Shuford, Deanne Shuford, Elaine Thompson, and Pamella Wilson. Diane Arkins, vintage Halloween expert, contributed the information and photography on pages 51–57.

For contributing carved pumpkins, thanks to Tim Daly, Sally Krahl, Chris Rich, Nicole Tuggle, and Skip Wade. The following generously allowed us to photograph at their homes or businesses: Carol Adams (at The Hill House Bed & Breakfast), Chris Bryant, April Carder, Scott Corley, Pat Lytle, Skip Wade, Glenn Whisman, and the staff of The Thomas Wolfe House, all in Asheville, North Carolina. Thanks especially to Tim and Marianna Daly for letting us in on their amazing annual pumpkin-carving event.

In addition, I would like to extend my appreciation to the models: Shane Alexander, William Allen, Jango Ballentine, Butch Bassett, Naomi Brown, Evans Carter, Susan Edwards, Celeste Gardner, Zachary Griffin, Andrea Jernigan, Thames Kaderabek, William Lawrence, Austin Letson, Hank Marshall, Tiffany Marshall, Beck Miller, Tamara Miller, Mercedes Rios-Young, Heather Smith, Timothy Taylor, Carla Weiss, and Jessamyn Weiss.

Finally, a big thank you to Catharine Sutherland, who wrote the ghost stories on pages 20, 88, 98, 110, 120, and 144 (and who was otherwise indispensable); to Heather Smith—her creative energy and hours of assistance were essential to the project; and to Chris Bryant, the art director, and Evan Bracken, the photographer, for making this project so much fun—and look so great.

…ar. The days become
…is a wonderful crisp-
…o change their color
…he earth into a spec-
…ands pop up along
…hearty stews, won-
…pie, and steaming
…pulled out of stor-
…n are lit.

…hts turn to keep-
…een. The tradi-
…ent Celts; they
…ar to the next
…alloween his-
…s last harvest
…es that have
…ms, such as

…joyed by
…heir cos-
…f candy.
…treats,
…their
…seeds

Introduction

Fall is a magical time of ye[ar]
shorter and cooler, and there
ness in the air. Leaves begin
and fall to the ground, turning
tacular tapestry. Fall produce s
roadsides. Autumn meals feature
derful fall vegetables, pumpkin
apple cider. Favorite sweaters are
age, and the first fires of the seaso

As summer turns to winter, our thoug
ing warm, and, of course, to Hallow
tion of Halloween began with the anci
celebrated the transition from one ye
on October 31 (see page 12 for more H
tory). Today, the abundance of the year
is celebrated in conjunction with activit
developed out of traditional Celtic custo
pumpkin carving and trick-or-treating.

Halloween has become a holiday that is e
people of all ages. Children contemplate t
tumes and look forward to scoring lots o
Adults decorate their homes, stock
plan parties, and read scary ghost st
young ones. Pumpkins are carved, pumpkin
toasted, and porches decorated.

This book is a comprehensive guide to Halloween, including everything from information on growing pumpkins to transforming your yard into a spooky graveyard to baking delicious Halloween cookies. Consequently, there are a wide variety of projects in this book, utilizing a range of techniques, from painting to cooking to floral design. They all have in common a basic skill level and a playful, often humorous approach to the holiday.

In addition, the book is packed with fascinating Halloween-related facts and information, such as the reasons behind the superstition of black cats, a brief look at historical witch-hunts, and tips for enjoying a safe Halloween. Halloween is a holiday with revellry, gaiety, and fantasy at its core. Here's to many such Halloweens to come!

History of Halloween

THE WORD HALLOWEEN was adapted from All Hallow's Eve, a holy evening that was observed in medieval England on October 31, the eve of All Saint's Day. Nonetheless, most of the customs we associate with Halloween date back to pre-Christianity. The first Halloween celebrations were held more than 2,000 years ago by the Celts, who lived in what is now England, Ireland, Scotland, Wales, and northern France.

Ancient Celts organized their year according to the agricultural calendar. They celebrated the changing of the seasons in conjunction with harvest times. The Celts organized *Samhain* around the last harvest season of the year; the word means "end of summer" and is pronounced "sow-in," with *sow* rhyming with *cow*. This celebration was the most important festival of the year for pagan Celts. Samhain was the observance of the Celtic New Year, which began November 1, and it symbolized the end of harvest and the beginning of the winter season. According to Celtic custom, Samhain did not begin until the sun set on October 31.

For the pre-Christian Celts, the transition from one year to the next (marking the beginning of diminishing sunlight) had an element of fear, since they believed this was the time when the people who had died in the previous year came back to be among the living. The barriers between this world and the world of the dead were removed for a short period and, until dawn, dead souls were free to roam. The Celts did not believe in demons or devils as such at this time. The dead spirits, however, were often considered hostile and dangerous; they were resentful toward the living, who were enjoying the land and bounty of the dead. It was thought that on Halloween night, these hostile spirits would try to trick humans into becoming lost in the fairy mounds, where they would be trapped indefinitely.

In order to disguise themselves from the evil spirits, people who went out on Halloween would paint their faces with soot. To appease the dead souls, food would be left on the steps and porches of their houses, in the hopes that the spirits would take the food and leave without bringing them harm. Often, bonfires were lit to frighten off any demons or ghosts. In this way, people hoped to escape the dead spirits and gain safe passage into the new year.

One legend held that on Halloween night, graves opened up and corpses emerged. The corpses would commune amongst each other in the graveyard. If any living person witnessed this event, he or she was doomed to die or become mad.

Simple soot-faced disguises evolved into more elaborate costumes (often costumes of the opposite sex), and people began traveling from house to house, accepting food, even dancing or singing as they passed. Eventually, it became the custom to dress as skeletons and ghosts—imitations of the spirits themselves—and go door to door for treats. It also became common for pranks (sometimes of a malicious nature, which were supposedly the acts of the spirits) to be played on Halloween night. Young boys, in particular, would roam the neighborhoods, breaking windows and overturning outhouses.

Though there was an element of fear, the Celts generally regarded Halloween night as one of merrymaking, superstition, fortune-telling, and feasting. Halloween was thought to be a good time for seeing into the future, with respect to marriage, health, and luck. In Scotland, young people would gather for games to determine which among them would marry in the coming year.

A traditional Irish dish called *callcannon* was frequently served on Halloween night. It was made from mashed potatoes, parsnips, and onions, and a ring, a china doll, a thimble, and a coin were stirred into the mixture. The person who received the ring in their portion was to be married in the coming year; a thimble meant a lifetime of bachelorhood. A china doll in the callcannon meant the person would have children. And, of course, whoever was fortunate to get the coin would have wealth. A similar tradition involved baking a ring and a nut in a cake. The finder of the ring would marry; the finder of the nut would marry a widow or widower. That is, unless the latter found the nut's kernel shriveled, in which case he or she could never expect to marry at all.

During the Middle Ages, Halloween became known as the Night of the Witch. Witchcraft was an organized cult at this time, which was opposed to the Roman Catholic Church, and Halloween night was set aside as a day in which the devil and his witches and demons gathered to meet. These unholy beings would mock the coming of the Church's festival of All Saints' Day, or November 1. On All Saints' Day, the church honored any saints who did not have a church holiday of their own. Establishing All Saints' Day, to a large degree, was an effort to create a religious celebration in reaction to the pagan holiday. In spite of the Church's efforts, people continued to celebrate the night before, and the holiday became known as All Hallows' Eve, and eventually, Halloween.

Because of the failure of the potato crop in Ireland (1845–1850), many Irish people, modern-day descendants of the Celts, immigrated to the United States, bringing with them their cultural practices. Since then, Halloween has developed into a major secular holiday, and a number of the Celtic Halloween traditions survive to this day.

devilish
decorations

designer: **KIM TIBBALS-THOMPSON**

Bat Table Runner

Black bats and a bewitching full moon adorn this imaginative table runner. Though this project requires a fair number of materials, it is sure to be a Halloween decoration you'll cherish for years to come.

creepy cobwebs

White cotton cheesecloth makes great cobwebs. Use a craft knife to make slits in the cheesecloth, then hang from ceilings, railings, and furniture.

What You Need

- Piece of blue felt, 5 feet x 20 inches (1.5 m x 51 cm) for top piece
- Piece of blue felt, 5 feet x 22 inches (1.5 m x 56 cm) for bottom piece
- ⅓ yard (.3 m) of 72-inch-wide (183-cm) black felt
- Scrap of dark gold felt
- Scrap of yellow felt
- Patterns for bat and moon (on this page)
- Gold acrylic craft paint
- Wooden stars in assorted sizes, approximately 35
- 16 small black buttons or beads (for bat eyes)
- Gold thread
- Gold embroidery thread
- Pinking shears
- Sewing machine
- Electric drill

ENLARGE MOON DRAWING 285%

What You Do

Use pinking shears to cut out the felt pieces according to the patterns provided. Photocopy the bat pattern at different percentages to create bats in assorted sizes. The moon, bats, and stars will be sewn to one piece of blue felt; the bottom piece serves as an extra layer and to cover the stitching underneath the top piece. Taper the short sides of the blue felt pieces, using the photograph (page 14) as a guide. Note that the top of the moon and the largest bat extend beyond the top piece of blue felt; the bottom piece should be cut with matching extended areas. In this way, you will not have to stitch through three layers of felt in those areas. Transfer the moon face design onto the gold and yellow felt.

. . . .

Using the photograph as a guide, place all fabric pieces on the top piece of blue felt and pin. Machine stitch around the outside edge (not including the extension piece) of the dark gold piece of moon first, as it will lie underneath the yellow piece. As you work, stitch around the face design where possible. Stitch the yellow piece on next, again working face design. Once the moon is in place, complete the outline of the face design with machine stitching, and fill in design with gold acrylic craft paint.

. . . .

Next, stitch on the bats, beginning with the smallest bat (near the moon) and working your way across. Remember not to stitch all the way around the largest bat that extends off the edge of the runner yet. Stitch on small buttons or beads for bat eyes. Drill a hole in about 25 of the wooden stars and paint each star with gold acrylic paint. Sew the stars onto the runner in a random pattern with gold embroidery thread.

. . . .

Once all the pieces are stitched in place, position the top (design) layer of blue felt on top of the bottom layer (with the extensions). To make the tassel-like embellishments for each end, paint the other 10 stars with gold paint, then drill a hole in the top of each. Tie a length of six strands of embroidery thread to each star, cut the thread to varying lengths, and sandwich the strands between the two pieces of blue felt as you topstitch the outer edges. Topstitch around the entire outside edge of the table runner.

Bats

BATS ARE THE only flying mammals; most bats eat fruit, flower nectar, insects, frogs, or fish. In many areas, bat habitation is encouraged, because bats can drastically reduce insect populations.

So why do bats have such a bad reputation? Perhaps it comes partly from the vampire bat, which gets its nourishment from the blood of other living creatures—an admittedly creepy feeding habit. In some parts of the world, bats were said to be the form souls of the dead took to roam about at night. Others thought that bats were actually the Devil—out to spy among the living—or forms of witches or vampires. (Bram Stoker's *Dracula* did much to reinforce the notion that vampires and bats were interchangeable.)

Though many people still fear bats, the bat is actually a good luck omen in China and Poland. In fact, to the Chinese, the bat symbolizes a long and happy life. In addition, one British superstition claims that a bat spotted in bad weather means that fair weather is coming soon.

designer: **GINGER SUMMIT**

Gourd Table Pumpkins

Position a string of lights underneath these cute little gourd pumpkins to create an impressive centerpiece for a table filled with Halloween goodies. Fill them with candy and pass them out to friends and neighbors as a gesture of affection.

What You Need

- Miniature round ornamental gourds, cured and cleaned
- Pencil
- Craft knife or wood-burning tool
- Leather dye or watered-down acrylic paint, orange
- Orange raffia
- Hot-glue gun

What You Do

Cured gourds are widely available year-round at farmers' markets and floral supply stores. Small or ornamental gourds are among the most commonly sold gourd varieties.

········

Draw a jagged line (see photograph) around the top of each gourd, as well as a small hole in the bottom (for the lights), and carefully cut top and bottom holes out with a craft knife or a wood-burning tool. Clean the pulp and seeds from the inside of the gourd. Sketch jack-o'-lantern faces on the pumpkin gourds, and use the craft knife or a wood-burning tool to cut design out.

········

Paint the gourds (and the tops) with orange leather dye or watered-down acrylic paint, and allow to dry thoroughly. Tie a ribbon with orange raffia and hot-glue to the top of each pumpkin.

Old Raw Head

believable blood

A great alternative to store-bought "blood"—which is widely available, but rather expensive—is this simple recipe. Add red food coloring to light corn syrup until a deep red is achieved, then add several drops of blue food coloring for a crimson-colored goo. The "blood" is edible, so it's perfect dripping from a vampire's mouth.

BACK IN A DEEP, DARK, WOODED HOLLOW of the Ozark Mountains once stood a dilapidated cabin where an old, wise woman made her home. She spent her days using roots and herbs to make magic spells. Only one (albeit unlikely) "friend" ever came to visit her—a hungry, vicious, wild razorback hog that rooted through her garbage for kitchen scraps. The mountain people said he was so full of roots and magic potions from her garbage, he could sing and dance just like a human. But other people said that was just talk.

Every October, when the leaves turned colors and the wind blew cold, the mountain people came together and rounded up their hogs for slaughter. After butchering the hogs and packing the meat into large burlap sacks, the farmers headed for home, where they would store the meat in a smokehouse for the winter. The only thing they left in the pens were piles of raw-skinned hog heads and bloody bones.

One year at hog-scalding time, a lazy hillbilly stole his neighbors' hogs, including the wild razorback hog, and butchered them in his pen. At the end of the day, as the sun went down, the lazy hillbilly loaded his wagon with a burlap sack full of meat and one raw-skinned hog head, and started for home. A few miles down the road, his wagon hit a bump, and the old raw head rolled onto the dark road.

Immediately, the old raw head sang out, "Bloody bones, get up and dance!"

The bloody bones lying in the dirt of the butchering pen jumped up and danced in circles, then came together and ran as fast as they could to Old Raw Head. Old Raw Head ran away into the dark and gathered things to wear from all the critters in the forest: the panther's fangs, the bear's claws, and the raccoon's tail. Then he set out for the lazy hillbilly's house.

The lazy hillbilly sat straight up in bed when he heard a loud, scratching sound in the chimney and saw bright orange sparks scatter in the fireplace. Slowly, he made his way over the cold, dark cabin floor to the fireplace, and came closer and closer until at last he could peek up the chimney. And there, looking down at him from the top of the chimney, sat the most vicious, terrifying wild razorback hog he had ever seen.

"Well, hog, what have you got those big old eyes for?" he asked in a shaky voice.

"To see your grave," the creature said in a low, rumbling voice.

"Well, hog, what've you got those great big claws for?" he asked, peering up the chimney.

"To dig your grave," said the deep, rumbling voice.

"Well, hog, what have you got that big, bushy tail for?" the old hillbilly asked, his entire body shaking now.

"To sweep your grave," said the dark, terrible voice, rumbling so loudly that the house shook.

The lazy hillbilly ran and hid under the bed and said, "Well, hog, what've you got those long sharp teeth for?"

"To eat you up!" said Old Raw Head, as he scrambled down the chimney and gobbled up the old man. Then he stole the hillbilly's shirt and overalls, and rode away on the man's horse.

Now the mountain people say that, every year on Halloween, you can still see Old Raw Head riding the horse deep in the Ozark Mountains, his eyes blazing like fire, and his raw-skinned head silhouetted against the full moon.

Yard Gravestones

*If you've always yearned
to turn your yard into an eerie
graveyard for Halloween,
then you're in luck; all you need
to make remarkably convincing
gravestones is polystyrene
(or insulating) board, paint,
and a few simple tools.*

designer: **PAMELLA WILSON**

What You Need

- Pieces of polystyrene board or insulating board in assorted sizes
- Acrylic paint, white, black, and gray
- Wire (optional)
- 5-inch (12.5-cm) bamboo stakes, a least two per gravestone
- Wood glue
- Spray bottle
- Steak knife
- Rasp
- Wood-burning tool or other blunt tool

What You Do

The size and shape of your gravestones will depend, to some degree, on the polystyrene or insulating board you have available. If the board is not thick enough to stand alone (most will not be), glue the pieces together with wood glue and allow to dry thoroughly. (A hot-glue gun will burn through the board.)

• • • • •

For each gravestone, you will need to build a foundation by gluing together several pieces of board. Anchor the grave stone to the foundation with wire, if necessary. (This is especially useful with taller gravestones.) Use a steak knife and a rasp to shape the board. Experiment with shapes and sizes, and vary the look of each gravestone.

just in case

People were so afraid of being buried alive in the 19th century that coffins were invented with an emergency air supply and an alarm system.

The stones are painted with watered-down acrylic paint; transfer paint to spray bottle and spray gravestones for a speckled, weathered effect. For best results, use combinations of black, gray, and white paint. Allow to dry thoroughly. A wood-burning tool is perfect for making lettering on the gravestones, but any blunt tool (a pen or even a stick) will work.

· · · · · · · ·

To anchor the gravestones into the ground, stick 5-inch (12.5-cm) bamboo stakes (available at floral supply stores) into the board, then into the ground. Two per piece should be enough, but additional stakes may be necessary for larger gravestones.

Black Cats

IF YOU COUNT a black cat among your companions, chances are you get a little nervous around Halloween. Floyd Wade keeps a cautious eye on his yellow-eyed black cat in October. "I try to never let Chelsea out of my sight around Halloween. People are really afraid of black cats, and I've heard teenagers kidnap them for pranks. It scares me, to say the least."

Why are people so superstitious about black cats? It has not always been the case. In ancient Egypt, any cats, regardless of color, were held as sacred creatures and worshipped in religious ceremonies. The Egyptians loved their cats immensely, and Egyptian cats were probably history's most well-treated cats. When a cat died, in fact, it was common for everyone in the household to shave their eyebrows in mourning—and cats were mummified.

But during the Middle Ages, the friendly and much-revered feline ran out of luck. Medieval people had a natural distrust of the unknown and perceived cats as mysterious—primarily, it seems, because they were nocturnal. Some even believed that cats were liaisons between witches and the devil, and that witches were capable of taking the form of a black cat when

necessary. Cats whose eyes were in greatest contrast to their fur—black cats— were thought to be followers of witches and evil spirits. During the witch trials in America and Europe, cats were frequently tortured and killed for their believed associations with witches.

Before long, the poor black cat was blamed for all manner of unfortunate accidents and unexplained mishaps, and a superstition of all black cats became deeply ingrained. It was believed that if a black cat crossed a person's path, that person had made a pact with the devil and would see bad luck in the coming year. While there has been much bad-luck lore associated with the black cat, sailors have long believed that a black cat kept on board their ship would ensure a safe voyage; their wives often kept one at home as well—just for good measure.

Even today, black cats suffer unduly for their fur color. Animal shelters report difficulty placing black cats, because people fear they will bring bad luck, and often these unfortunately colored creatures are put to death—without so much as a shaved eyebrow.

What You Need

- 18- x 12-inch (45.5- x 30.5-cm) piece of 1-inch-thick (2.5-cm) wood
- ¼-inch (.5-cm) dowel rod, 4 inches (10 cm) long
- 5-inch (12.5-cm) polystyrene ball
- 1 pair of toddler shoes, size 2 to 4
- 1 pair of toddler pants, size 24 months to 3T
- Polyester filling
- White sheeting fabric, approximately 2 yards (1.8 m)
- Twine
- Black felt
- Halloween ribbon, hairpin for girl; small baseball cap for boy
- Small plastic pumpkin container
- Skill saw or other wood-cutting tool
- Wood glue
- White craft glue
- Hot-glue gun

What You Do

Use a skill saw or other wood-cutting tool to cut wood block into a rough body form as illustrated, or have the form cut at a local lumber yard. Cut two 2½-inch (6.5-cm) pieces for the feet and glue to the bottom of the form with wood glue.

. . . .

In the center at the top of the wood form, drill a ¼-inch (.5-cm) hole about 2 inches (5 cm) deep. Place wood glue in hole and insert dowel rod into hole. (The dowel rod will stabilize the foam ball.) Push polystyrene ball onto dowel rod. Place white craft glue between ball and wood form to secure ball in place.

. . . .

Put shoes on wooden feet and tie laces tightly. Place pants on body form, and stuff pants with polyester stuffing to fill out legs. Place extra stuffing in the rear. (If pants are too long, fold pants at shoe level.) Place stuffing around foam head, making sure you keep the form smooth.

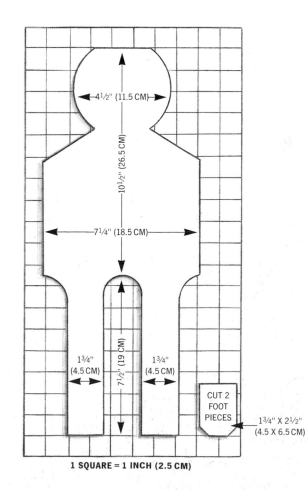

4½" (11.5 CM)
10½" (26.5 CM)
7¼" (18.5 CM)
1¾" (4.5 CM) 7½" (19 CM) 1¾" (4.5 CM)
CUT 2 FOOT PIECES 1¾" X 2½" (4.5 X 6.5 CM)

1 SQUARE = 1 INCH (2.5 CM)

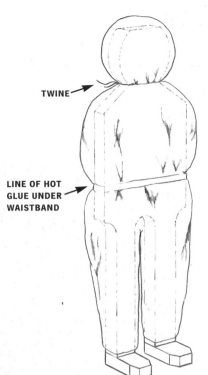

TWINE

**LINE OF HOT
GLUE UNDER
WAISTBAND**

Cut a 24-inch (61-cm) square piece from the white sheeting fabric and drape over head. Tie a piece of twine around neck area to secure stuffing and fabric. Place stuffing around upper body form as well, and take excess white fabric (from the head area) and insert into top of pants to form the upper body. Use hot-glue gun to make a line of glue inside the waistband of the pants to secure pants and stuffing.

. . . .

Cut a round piece of white sheet fabric with a 34-inch (86.5-cm) diameter. Fold circle of material in half and establish center of the circle. Cut two 1-inch (2.5-cm) circles out of the black felt for the eyes. Glue circles to material, approximately 12 inches (30.5 cm) from the edge of the circle and about 1 inch (2.5 cm) apart.

. . . .

Put a small amount of white craft glue on the top of the head and center sheet on head. Press on glued portion several seconds to secure. (Before gluing, make sure eyes are level and centered in front.) Sew trick-or-treat pumpkin container to sheet in front of doll. If you are making little boys, hot-glue cap on head; for a girl, attach a bow or ribbon to head, if desired.

alternative treats

This year, try handing out unexpected treats that will not give trick-or-treaters a sugar high. Kids will enjoy rubber stamps, stickers, temporary tattoos, and colorful pencils, for example, long after candy is gone.

Photograph taken at the home of Neal and Pam Beattie, Candler, North Carolina.

Mr. and Mrs. Ghost

*You'll find this delightful ghost couple a wonderful addition to your Halloween decor;
they are quite happy on the mantel, by your front door, or even outdoors. Place a
flashlight inside them, and they will serve as a shining welcome for trick-or-treaters.*

designer: **GINGER SUMMIT**

What You Need

- 2 bottle-type gourds, cured and cleaned (see below)
- Miniature basket-type gourd, cured and cleaned (see below)
- Craft knife or keyhole saw
- Wood-burning tool (optional)
- Toothpicks
- Pencil
- Leather dye or watered-down acrylic paint, white and orange
- Paintbrush
- Black permanent marker
- Small piece of black twine
- Hot-glue gun
- Accessories: small top hat and bow tie for Mr. Ghost; hat and necklace for Mrs. Ghost

ghosts with a message

Some believe that certain ghosts appear for the purpose of warning family members of impending danger and/or to demand vengeance. Such was the case with one of literature's most famous ghosts, in Shakespeare's play *Hamlet*. Hamlet's father, the murdered king of Denmark, appears in the play to reveal his murderer and implore his son, Hamlet, to avenge his death.

✝

What You Do

Cured gourds are widely available year-round at farmers' markets and floral supply stores. Bottle-type gourds come in many shapes and sizes. Pick two gourds that are shaped somewhat like bowling pins. You will also need a miniature basket-type gourd, such as an ornamental gourd, for Mr. Ghost's jack-o'-lantern container.

• • • • • • • •

Draw a jagged line (see photograph on page 31) around the bottom of each large gourd and carefully cut bottom out with a craft knife or keyhole saw. Clean the inside of the the pulp and seeds.

• • • • • • • •

Soak the large gourds in water for 15 minutes, then use a craft knife or a wood-burning tool to cut two arm-like slits in each gourd. Use your fingers to gently pull the arms away from the body of the gourd, and wedge toothpicks between the arms and body. Allow to dry with toothpicks in place, then remove toothpicks.

• • • • • • • •

Sketch eyes and mouth on the gourds (and a nose, if you wish), and use the craft knife or a wood-burning tool to cut these out. (A wood-burning tool works better for detail work.) Paint the large gourds with white leather dye or watered-down acrylic paint, and allow to dry thoroughly.

• • • • • • • •

Cut the top out of the miniature gourd with a craft knife or wood-burning tool. Paint the gourd with orange leather dye or watered-down acrylic paint, and allow to dry thoroughly. Draw a jack-o'-lantern face on the gourd, and hot-glue a piece of black twine to the gourd for a hanger.

• • • • • • • •

Next, "dress" Mr. and Mrs. Ghost with accessories of your choice. Here, the designer has constructed a small top hat out of black felt and hot-glued a bow tie in place at the neck for Mr. Ghost; and adorned Mrs. Ghost with a string of faux pearls and a hat.

• • • • • • • •

NOTE: Do not place a candle inside these gourds, as it may pose a safety hazard; use a flashlight instead.

The Pink Lady
of the Grove Park Inn

THE MYSTERY OF THE PINK LADY has perplexed employees and guests of the historic Grove Park Inn, a grand old hotel in Asheville, North Carolina, for decades. Legend has it that a young lady dressed in pink fell to her death from an indoor balcony in the Palm Court atrium sometime around 1920—and has been haunting the hotel ever since.

For more than half a century, the Pink Lady has been seen or felt by a number of unsuspecting visitors. She has been sighted throughout the Main Inn of this charming hotel, a structure noted for its high stone walls and giant fireplaces. It seems these paranormal sightings have been concentrated in the area of Room 545, two stories above the floor of the

Palm Court atrium. Dozens of employees and guests, many of whom had no knowledge of the Pink Lady legend, have described having cold chills and hair-raising experiences near Room 545, or have reported actually seeing the faint impression of a woman dressed in pink in the vicinity.

In 1996, the inn mounted an in-depth study of the Pink Lady phenomenon, which included scientific fieldwork, investigative reporting, and interviews. Those who have seen the Pink Lady say she is a gentle ghost, albeit a sad one. Though it is still unclear why or even exactly when the Pink Lady fell to her death, she is believed by many to be a permanent guest at the Grove Park Inn.

Skull
Paper Banner

In Mexico, bright strands of papel picado, *or Mexican papercutting, are hung from ceilings or in plazas or streets. This skull and crossbones version makes a colorful indoor Halloween decoration.*

What You Need

- Tissue paper in Halloween colors, at least 3 sheets, approximately 8½ x 11 inches (21.5 x 28 cm) each
- Paper clips
- Small scissors with sharp blades or a craft knife (optional)
- Cardboard
- Additional sheets of uncut tissue paper
- Iron
- String or twine
- Glue stick

designer: **KATHLEEN TRENCHARD**

What You Do

Photocopy the pattern provided on page 35. Stack colored pieces of tissue—here, we've used orange and black—and fold stack in half widthwise. Fold the pattern, place on top of the stack, match the center of the pattern with the fold of the tissues, and attach the pattern to the stack of tissue with paper clips. (Do not use tape; it will tear the paper.)

⋯⋯⋯

Carefully cut out the black spaces. Use scissors to cut out the curved shapes and outside sections; use a craft knife (against cardboard) to cut cut the inside black spaces or fold on the dotted lines, and cut the inside shapes out. Remove the pattern and unfold the tissue paper.

Separate the sheets of cut tissue. Iron the paper between two sheets of uncut tissue, using a hot setting.

⋯⋯⋯

Arrange the pieces of paper in a row on a flat surface. There should be at least an inch (2.5 cm) separating each banner from the one next to it. Cut enough string to span the arrangement, leaving at least a foot (.3 m) of string at either end for installation. Apply glue (with a glue stick) about ½ inch (1.5 cm) from the top across each piece of tissue paper. Gently fold the top of the tissue over the string, pressing the tissues together. Allow glue to dry at least five minutes before hanging.

ENLARGE DRAWING 170%

everyone's included

In Mexico on All Hallows' Day or the Day of the Dead (November 1), families take food to the graves of dead relatives and engage in merry feasting—making it a celebration that *everyone* can enjoy.

Painted Pumpkins

Paint markers are available at craft supply stores in a variety of colors and make painting pumpkins easy and fun—a great project for young children. Feel free to paint traditional jack-o'-lantern faces on your pumpkins; here the designer has chosen his favorite Halloween creatures.

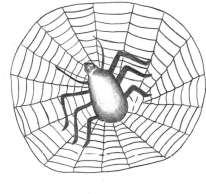

What You Need

- Sugar pumpkins or pie pumpkins
- Paint markers in assorted colors
- Clear shellac
- Cotton swabs
- Rubbing alcohol

What You Do

Wash pumpkin thoroughly and dry with a clean cloth. Either use the patterns provided to transfer the design onto the pumpkin with a light pen or pencil, or free-hand the design straight onto the pumpkin with the paint markers. The paint is easily removed with rubbing alcohol, so don't worry about getting it perfect the first time around. Once you have completed the design, go over it again with the paint markers to achieve a deeper color.

. . . .

When you have finished painting, use a cotton swab dipped in alcohol to clean up the design. Allow the paint to dry for at least one hour, then spray clear shellac over the entire pumpkin. Allow to dry thoroughly. **NOTE:** The paint will come off if the pumpkin bumps against other objects. If this happens, simply use the paint marker to touch up design as needed.

Frankenstein

One of literature's most frightening monsters comes from a best-selling book published in 1818. *Frankenstein* was written by Mary Wollstonecraft Shelley, wife of the famous romantic poet, Percy Shelley. In the tale, a scientist named Frankenstein creates the monster; eventually, the creature turns to violence out of frustration from the isolation he feels. The American film *Frankenstein* was released in 1931, featuring Boris Karloff as the monster. Film-goers were impressed with the story and began to call the heretofore unnamed monster Frankenstein. The misnomer has stuck ever since.

Growing Pumpkins

FIRST, you should determine what variety of pumpkins you desire. Carving pumpkins tend to be watery and bland, but are usually quite symmetrical and flat on the bottom. Good cooking pumpkins have a sweet, firm, smooth-textured flesh, but don't necessarily carve well.

Pumpkins require rich, well-drained soil (deep loam is preferred) with a pH of between 6.0 and 6.5. (They will, however, tolerate slightly more acidic soil.) Pumpkins are extremely frost-tender and need moderate amounts of water. They are a long-seasoned crop, usually requiring 90 to 120 growing days (depending on the variety and the temperature). Pumpkin plants will need some wind protection and plenty of space to grow.

Ideally, you should begin to cultivate the soil a year in advance. The preferred method is to dig in plenty of compost and aged manure to the soil the autumn before you plan to plant. You can also prepare the soil just before planting.

Usually, the soil is warm enough for planting pumpkins by May. That being said, be careful not to plant too early. If you want your pumpkins to be ready around Halloween, July is usually the best time. The seeds need a temperature of 60°F (16°C) to sprout. Two rules of thumb: Plant pumpkins when the blackberries begin to bloom, and if the soil is warm enough to sprout corn, it's warm enough to sprout pumpkins.

If you live in regions with a short growing season, start the pumpkin seeds indoors no more than two weeks before the last expected frost date. It's a good idea to cover your pumpkin plot with black plastic when you plant the seeds to ensure the ground will be warm enough to plant the seedlings. Plant seeds in 3-inch (7.5-cm) peat pots, then plant seedlings outdoors in three to four weeks. Do not let the roots become too extensive (and certainly not root-bound) before you transplant the pumpkin seedlings.

Pumpkins grow best when planted in beds, which prevents flooding. Before you plant pumpkins in your garden, work high-nitrogen fertilizer into the soil. Space seeds or seedlings in groups with 6 to 8 feet (2 to 2.5 m) between each group.

As they grow and begin to crowd each other, thin the plants until there are only two or three of the strongest plants left. Turn the tips of the pumpkin vines in the direction you want them to grow. Fertilize the growing plants with diluted fish emulsion, rotted manure, or compost every three weeks, and keep the soil evenly moist. When pumpkins begin to form, place sand or a board underneath to prevent decay. Prevent flattening on sides by turning the pumpkins periodically. (Be careful not to break or bend the brittle vine.)

Harvest pumpkins when skin is firm and the stem has hardened. Store pumpkins in a warm, well-ventilated area for several weeks, then transfer them to a cool, dry place.

Spooky Spoon Centerpiece

*This unusual arrangement is adorned with mismatched vintage spoons,
which can be found in plentiful supply (and for very little money) at
thrift stores. Wrap the twigs and branches with small white string lights
for a particularly frightening effect. These painted spoons also make fun
Halloween necklaces; slip the bent spoon on a ribbon or a chain.*

What You Need

- Assorted spoons, approximately 15
- Gesso
- Acrylic paint, orange
- Fabric paint, black and green
- Medium pumpkin
- Block of polystyrene
- Assorted twigs, branches, and vines
- Hot-glue gun (optional)
- Spanish moss and/or dried leaves

designer: **TAMARA MILLER**

What You Do

Hold each spoon with beveled side (or back of spoon)
facing you, and gently bend the handle toward you so
that both the decorative side of the handle and the
beveled side are facing outward. Paint the back of each
spoon with gesso to create a base on which to paint. Allow
to dry thoroughly. Paint the pumpkin shape on each
spoon first with orange acrylic paint, and allow to dry
thoroughly. Create details and jack-o'-lantern faces with
black and green fabric paint.

● ● ● ● ● ● ●

Carve the top out of the pumpkin and clean out seeds
and pulp. Cut a polystyrene block to fit inside pumpkin,
and press ends of twigs and vines in foam. A dab of hot
glue will hold these materials more securely. Arrange
Spanish moss or dried leaves around the base of the
arrangement, and hang spoons from twigs and vines.

that's a big pumpkin!

The world's largest pumpkin was grown by Nathan
and Paul Zehr in Lowville, New York, in 1996.
It weighed 1,061 pounds (481 kg).

designer: **PERRI CRUTCHER**

Welcoming Topiaries

At Halloween, it's important that your porch become an inviting, pleasing area of your home. These topiaries accomplish just that when placed on either side of an outside entryway.

What You Need (for one topiary)

- Three 6-foot (1.8-m) wooden branches/sticks, approximately 3 inches (7.5 cm) in diameter each
- Floral wire
- Six pieces of wood, approximately 6 x 2 inches (15 x 5 cm)
- Floral foam
- Chicken wire
- One small bag of cement or blocks of polystyrene
- 20-inch (51-cm) terra-cotta pot
- Green sheet moss
- Floral picks
- Weathered boxwood
- Colorful leaves with partial branches
- Cotton bows, sprayed with weather guard
- Hammer and nails
- Hot-glue gun (optional)

a goblin by any other name

The word goblin comes from French folklore. These ghostly creatures were believed to be mysterious spirits who inhabited households (especially those with beautiful children and lots of wine), both helping (by doing chores at night, for example) and playing pranks on the residents. In England and Scotland, the same phenomenon is called a brownie; in Germany, a *kobald*; and in Russia, a *domovik*.

What You Do

Bind the three branches or sticks together with floral wire at the top, center, and bottom. Nail pieces of 6- x 2-inch (15- x 5-cm) wood to the top, center, and bottom of the wired branches (about 20 inches or 51 cm from the bottom of the branches), so that the pieces of wood are perpendicular to the branches.

....

Place two blocks of foam on each side of the pieces of wood, and wrap chicken wire around the foam to form three balls—try to create a 20-inch (51-cm) ball at the bottom, a 15-inch (38-cm) ball in the center, and a 10-inch (25.5-cm) ball at the top. Wind floral wire around each ball to secure.

....

Mix the cement according to the manufacturer's instructions. While holding the sticks in a vertical position, insert the bottom of the topiary (the bottom ends of the branches) into the pot you have selected, then fill pot with cement. Hold branches upright until cement sets. Allow the cement to dry thoroughly.

....

An alternative to cement is to use blocks of polystyrene. Wedge the polystyrene into the pot, and insert bottom end of topiary in the center of the pot. Cover the top of the cement or polystyrene with green sheet moss. Hot-glue moss in place, if necessary.

Next, attach floral picks to bunches of weathered boxwood, and insert into foam balls until all three balls are completely covered with boxwood. **NOTE:** For this project, boxwood should be harvested in the spring when it is dark green and allowed to age over the summer until it turns light brown.

•••••

Shape the autumn leaves into clusters by wrapping the stems with floral wire and attaching floral picks. Insert leaves (and any partial branches you have gathered) into the center and bottom balls, and secure with floral wire, if necessary.

•••••

Hand-tie a double-looped French bow with a piece of striped cotton cloth (or any other cloth of your choice) that has been sprayed with weather guard. (Weather guard is especially important if the topiary will be exposed to the weather.) Loop a length of floral wire through the back of the bows and attach a bow to the branches between the boxwood balls—two bows in all.

Harvest Porch Crate

A bundle of dried grasses, fresh Holland lilies, and spiky autumn berries make this porch arrangement a pleasingly dramatic outdoor decoration. A black-and-white striped ribbon is a nice, Halloween-inspired touch.

What You Need

- Wooden crate
- Floral foam
- Green sheet moss
- Floral pins
- Floral picks
- Dried hydrangea blooms
- Bundle of dried wild grasses and wheat
- Raffia
- Cotton bow, sprayed with weather guard
- Floral wire
- Fresh flowers
- Floral tubes
- Fresh nandin berries and bittersweet
- Small pumpkin
- Hot-glue gun (optional)

designer: **PERRI CRUTCHER**

What You Do

Choose a crate. This one is 14 x 6 x 10 inches (35.5 x 15 x 25.5 cm). Cut pieces of floral foam to fit inside the crate, with approximately 1 inch (2.5 cm) of foam extending beyond the crate. Wedge the foam into the crate, and cover the top of the foam with green sheet moss. Use floral pins to secure moss, if necessary. Attach floral picks to the stems of the dried hydrangeas and insert the picks into the floral foam, creating a cluster pattern in the front left and back right corner of the crate.

. . . .

Tie the bundle of dried grasses and wheat at the top and bottom with the raffia. Place the wheat diagonally across the center of the crate. Hand-tie a double-looped French bow with a piece of striped cotton cloth (or any other cloth of your choice) that has been sprayed with weather guard. (Weather guard is especially important if the crate will be exposed to the weather.) Loop a length of floral wire through the back of the bow, and attach bow to the bundle of grasses.

. . . .

Place the stems of the fresh flowers (here we've used Holland lilies) in floral tubes, and insert tubes into the floral foam throughout the arrangement to create a pleasing design. Insert nandin berries, bittersweet, or other berries into the back of the crate. Nestle a small pumpkin in the center of the design; hot-glue pumpkin in place, if necessary.

Pumpkin
Porch Crate

An unusually shaped pumpkin is the centerpiece for this porch crate,
and a stalk of winding bittersweet gives the piece an eerie, overgrown feel—
making it a perfect decoration for haunted-house season.

designer: **PERRI CRUTCHER**

What You Need

- Wooden crate
- Floral foam
- Green sheet moss
- Floral pins
- A large, uniquely shaped pumpkin
- Cotton bow, sprayed with weather guard
- Floral picks
- Dried hydrangea blooms
- Dried bittersweet
- Assorted autumn leaves and berries

What You Do

Choose a crate. This one is 14 x 6 x 10 inches (35.5 x 15 x 25.5 cm). Cut pieces of floral foam to fit inside the crate, with approximately 1 inch (2.5 cm) of foam extending beyond the crate. Wedge the foam into the crate, and cover the top of the foam with green sheet moss. Use floral pins to secure the moss, if necessary. Place the pumpkin in the center of the crate. It will probably not be necessary to secure the pumpkin, as it should rest securely in the center of the crate.

· · · · · · · ·

Hand-tie a double-looped French bow with a piece of striped cotton cloth (or any other cloth of your choice) that has been sprayed with weather guard. (Weather guard is especially important if the crate will be exposed to the weather.) Slip the cotton bow around the pumpkin's stem.

· · · · · · · ·

Attach floral picks to the stems of the bittersweet and dried hydrangea blooms, and insert the picks into the floral foam as desired to create a pleasing arrangement. Fill any spaces with autumn leaves and assorted berries by sticking branches and stems directly into the foam.

Glow-in-the-Dark Window Decorations

Greet your guests with these spooky window decorations. The designs are actually executed on wax paper (not on your window) ahead of time—experimenting with colors and styles is half the fun.

designer: **CHERYLE KINLEY**

What You Do

Fabric paint is available at craft stores in easy-to-use and inexpensive squeeze bottles. First, sketch a design on a piece of white typing paper with a pencil, then trace over the design with a heavy black marker. Lay a sheet of wax paper over the typing paper and trace over the design with fabric paint. (Using fabric paint bottles with small tips makes detail work easier.)

• • • • • • •

When using several colors, paint first with the color that covers the largest area (usually the yellow paint), allow to dry thoroughly, then use black or blue paint for accenting. **NOTE:** The thinner the coat of paint, the more easily the decorations stick to the window.

• • • • • • •

To mount decoration, wet the front of the design with a small amount of hot water (a small paintbrush works well for this purpose) and press decoration against clean window surface. Apply pressure for several seconds. The design will stay in place on window, but is easily removed.

What You Need

- White typing paper
- Pencil
- Heavy black marker
- Wax paper
- Glow-in-the-dark fabric paint (in yellow and blue)
- Black fabric paint

VINTAGE NOISEMAKERS AND PARTY HATS.
The cardboard horn, third from the left, dates to the 1920s; the others date to the 1940s/1950s.

Vintage
Halloween Collectibles

*It seems vintage Halloween memorabilia has become the rage
among collectors and Halloween enthusiasts. Here, expert collector
Diane Arkins offers her take on the newest antiquing craze.*

CUSTOMS surrounding the celebration of All Hallow's Eve, or Hallowe'en as it was commonly called, stem largely from old world traditions brought to America by the influx of Scottish and Irish immigrants during the mid-1800s.

By the early decades of the 20th century, observances of Halloween had grown to encompass a wide range of festivities—barn dances, church socials, club suppers, home parties, and the like—staged to both celebrate the harvest and provide properly chaperoned social gatherings for adults. It was these gala events that gave birth to the eclectic mix of Halloween paraphernalia cherished by contemporary collectors.

Among the most popular examples of Halloween memorabilia are vintage candy containers and lanterns. Variously manufactured of paper mache, "composition" (a form of paper mache to which plaster or sawdust has been added for durability), cardboard, tissue, and crepe papers, these lightweight creations gave festive form to traditional Halloween symbols, and, as the products of German cottage industry, their designs embodied a uniquely unrefined folk-artsy styling.

Halloween candy containers from the 1920s and 1930s often assumed the form of cats and harvest figures—mischievous imps with vegetable "heads"

ABOVE: German-made candy container from around 1900.

RIGHT: A rare pressed-cardboard cat-face lantern is of German origin and dates to 1910.

ABOVE: A weathered patina and menacing expression are hallmarks of this 1940s "egg-crate paper mache" cat lantern.

RIGHT: Paper mache lanterns like these were meant to hold lighted candles. The lantern at left still has its original tissue paper insert; the one at right shows flame and smoke damage, which was likely incurred when its insert caught fire.

and "limbs." (See page 56 to learn how to make such a figure.) Some of these whimsical characters were perched atop crudely decorated boxes; others were designed so that removing their heads—or a concealed plug—would reveal the sweets hidden within.

Halloween lanterns from the 1920s, 1930s, and 1940s were relatively fragile creations, which were commonly styled as grinning jack-o'-lanterns or rapscallious cat heads; examples of witch and devil heads are rarer finds. While larger lanterns existed, the bulk were typically 4 to 7 inches (10 to 18 cm) high, and their open facial features were backed with decorative tissue paper inserts intended to project an eerie glow when lit from within. Some lanterns bore well-merited warnings. One such note cautioned, "This toy has been treated with a solution that renders it slow burning in case, by accident, it ignites. The features can be illuminated by filling the depression in the center of bottom with melted wax, then press candle into wax and cool until candle is firmly held vertically." The comparatively relaxed tone of this caveat bespeaks the innocence of the era in which such quaint novelties were produced. Ultimately, lantern design components were amended to preclude the hazards inherent to their use with candles.

LEFT: This heavily embossed German die-cut measures just 4 inches (10 cm) in diameter and dates to around 1910.

RIGHT: Fabulous graphics adorn this 1920s lightweight cardboard cat-face garland.

Embossed cardboard, crepe, and tissue paper decorations were the staples of early Halloween events and are eagerly sought after by modern collectors. Early 20th-century party protocol dictated that virtually every available surface be recruited for decorating duty. Whether in the home or gathering hall, lamps, chandeliers, windows, and even mops and brooms were all bedecked with festive images of jack-o'-lanterns and "vegetable people," black cats and witches, ghosts and goblins. Lengths of heavy-duty crepe paper illustrated in repeating seasonal tableaux were used to outfit party tables as well as craft paper costumes meant to be worn over plain muslin frocks. Garlands constructed of cardboard Halloween cut-outs were used to drape everything from stage fronts to walls and curtains.

Among the myriad paper treasures sought after by collectors are crepe- or tissue-paper hats, invitations, place card markers, and handcrafted party favors, such as nut cups embellished with decorative gummed seals. Wall decorations made of die-cut cardboard, however, may well represent the pinnacle of Halloween paper collectibles. Especially popular are 1920s and 1930s German designs with embossing so deep their thick cardboard features boast an elegant dimensional feel. Grinning pumpkin-faced characters, cats with arched backs and menacing grins, owls, scarecrows, skeletons, and witches were popular motifs for die-cut decorations.

RIGHT: Tissue-paper party hats, ca. 1930

ABOVE: A pair of stunt board games are surrounded by early postcards and other vintage ephemera.

No night of Halloween revelry was complete without the noisemakers used to both guide home friendly spirits and frighten away those with ominous intent. Noisemakers came in a vast array of styles, from feather-trimmed paper blow-outs, cardboard horns, and wooden ratchets to metal tambourines and tin can rattles. The stage for the evening's entertainment was often set with the help of gaily illustrated stunt game boards. With the spin of a wheel, party guests could learn their fortune or be enticed to perform a silly stunt.

To help plan the perfect Halloween celebration, many early-20th-century hostesses turned to the "Bogie Books" and party magazines—paper guidebooks published by Dennison Manufacturing Company of Framingham, Massachusetts, to promote the company's line of party goods. Filled with lavish illustrations and peerless decorating and party-giving advice for events both large and small, these 24- to 32-page volumes joyously captured the spirit of Halloweens past—and rarely fail to tickle the fancy of Halloween devotees present.

America's "Golden Age" of illustrated holiday postcards coincided with the decades that produced the earliest Halloween collectibles; and today's collectors avidly seek cards, dating from 1900-1918, that bear fanciful imagery of Halloween pranks, characters, and fortune-telling rituals. Cards that have been sent through the mail are as desirable as those that have not, and, as an added bonus, often bear messages that offer collectors an intimate glimpse at life in a bygone era.

BELOW: Dennison "Bogie" books and Halloween party guides from the 1910s, 1920s, and 1930s are especially popular with collectors.

TOP OF PAGE: Boxed die-cut decorations and gummed seals were produced in the 1920s, and used as decorations on party favors and costumes.

Despite the overwhelming popularity of older Halloween memorabilia, party items from the 1950s and 1960s are also cherished by collectors—especially those who dreamily recall the novelties from their own childhoods. This category of relatively modern Halloween memorabilia spotlights figural candles, hard plastic novelties (from tiny figures used as cupcake decorations to candy containers shaped like witches on wheels), and disposable partyware, such as decorative paper plates, tablecloths, cups, and napkins.

Collectors of vintage Halloween items seek out and display these nostalgic collectibles year-round. The ever-increasing popularity of these quaint old treasures has contributed to both scarcity and rising prices in the collecting marketplace. At this stage, the bargain days of collecting vintage Halloween have clearly passed.

Nonetheless, collections can still be built through dedicated antiquing efforts. Dependable treasure-hunting techniques—scouring antique shops, shows, and flea markets—can be a particularly effective way for neophyte collectors to familiarize themselves with the look and feel of the old-fashioned treasures they seek. Given the almost insatiably high demand for vintage Halloween items, today's buyers need to educate themselves and beware unscrupulous sorts who would pass off reproductions as vintage pieces. (Such copies should not, however, be confused with the genuine folk art creations of modern artists who seek to reflect the beauty of vintage pieces in signed creations of their own.)

Modern armchair shoppers can explore an array of shopping avenues, from mail-order sales and auctions to placing advertisements in collecting periodicals. The computer age has given birth to on-line bulletin boards for collectors.

Experienced collectors advocate buying any collectible in as fine a condition as possible; but if an item speaks to you—especially if its price is right—you should not hesitate to add it to your collection simply because you love it. Buying solely for investment purposes can often lead to disappointment. Perhaps the best advice of all is to always buy from reputable dealers you can trust.

FOR MORE INFORMATION ON HALLOWEEN MEMORABILIA

Prices for popular collectibles often change as soon as they are "established," and Halloween memorabilia is no exception. While the values quoted in the following collectors' guides do not necessarily reflect up-to-date market prices for many items, the books are excellent visual and informational references for anyone interested in vintage Halloween.

CAMPANELLI, DAN AND PAULINE CAMPANELLI. ***Halloween Collectibles: A Price Guide.*** L-W BOOK SALES, 1995.

SCHNEIDER, STUART. ***Halloween in America: A Collector's Guide with Prices.*** SCHIFFER PUBLISHING LTD, 1995.

Halloween Veggie People

The period from 1900 to 1918 is known as the Golden Age of illustrated picture postcards. During this era, cards routinely traversed the mail, carrying routine news as often as holiday greetings to family and friends. Fanciful images of vegetable people appeared on hundreds of postcard designs—both nonseasonal and Halloween-related. These wonderful old-fashioned illustrations are the inspiration for these veggie folks, which are sure to brighten your own Halloween celebrations.

designer: **DIANE ARKINS**

What You Need

- Assorted pumpkins, winter squash, or gourds
- Dowel rod, ⅛- to ³⁄₁₆-inch (.3- to .5-cm) diameter
- Awl
- Hot-glue gun
- Tiny ears of Indian corn
- Dried kernels of feed corn
- Leaves
- Acorns
- Branches and seed pods
- Hay and grass
- Assorted decorative gourds
- Wooden toothpicks

What You Do

Veggie people can be made in any size desired so long as components are in proportion with each other. First, wash and dry pumpkins and gourds. Fruits should be at room temperature—cold surfaces will impair the ability of glue to bond components.

· · · · · · ·

Cut a length of dowel rod (3 to 4 inches or 7.5 to 10 cm is usually enough) to secure head and body pumpkins together. Trim stem from bottom pumpkin. (If it's nicely curved, stem can later be used as a mouth. Use an awl to poke a centered starter hole where the two fruits will be joined.

· · · · · · ·

Squeeze hot glue into one hole and insert dowel piece halfway. Cover remaining portion of rod with additional hot glue and insert second pumpkin on rod. Press fruits together for a minute to allow glue to harden.

Use appropriate amounts of hot glue to affix facial and body features. Most decorative accents can be glued directly to pumpkin surfaces; cut pieces of decorative squash should be joined to pumpkin using toothpick supports.

· · · · · · ·

Use ears of Indian corn for arms; individual kernels of field corn for buttons or facial features; leaves for hats and collars; acorns for facial features and buttons; branches and seed pods for arms and mouths; hay and grass for hair; and pieces of assorted decorative gourds for facial features. A trip to your own backyard is likely to uncover dozens of other possibilities!

· · · · · · ·

Veggie people will last longer when kept in cool conditions. Handle them with care so as not to dislodge decorative features or unintentionally separate heads from bodies.

the real dracula

Dracula was a real person who lived in the
15th century. Indeed, Dracula was the nickname given to
a ruthless Romanian prince who was known for impaling his
enemies on sharp stakes (thus explaining his other nickname,
"Vlad the Impaler"). When Bram Stoker, a British author, undertook
the project of writing a vampire story, he decided to base
his fictional vampire on the real-life prince.
Dracula was published in 1897.

designer: **KIM TIBBALS-THOMPSON**

designer: **JEAN WALL PENLAND**

Halloween Luminaries

*Luminaries are an easy and dramatic way
to light your driveway or walkway on Halloween
evening for your parade of trick-or-treaters.
A layer of tracing paper taped to the inside
of the bag diffuses the candlelight
and provides an extra glowing effect.*

What You Need

- Brown unprinted paper bags
- Cardboard or foam board
- Pencil
- Craft knife

- Tracing paper
- Tape
- Sand
- Small candles

What You Do

Any brown paper bag will work, as long as it is unprinted.
First, turn down the top of the bag about 2 inches (5 cm);
this gives the luminary a nice, neat rim and helps the bag
keep its shape.

• • • • • • •

Determine which side of the paper bag will be the front side.
Using a pencil, lightly draw a design on the bag. You can
either trace a Halloween motif from another source (possibly one from this book) or freehand a design, as the designer
has done here. Lettering works well, as does using the bags
to form a message that must be read in sequence.

• • • • • • •

Place a piece of cardboard or foam board inside the bag, and
use a craft knife to cut out the design. Be careful not to cut
through to the back of the bag. Remove the cardboard or
foam board. Cut pieces of tracing paper to fit against the
front of the bag and tape paper in place.

• • • • • • •

Place a scoop of sand in the bottom of the bag; this will make
the luminary sit flatly, and will give the candle a sturdy
base. The candle should be positioned in the middle of the
sand, well away from the sides of the bag.

Haunted House Lamp Shade

A lamp shade made out of bright orange paper and painted with a haunted house scene will glow when cut and pierced to allow light to shine through. Here, we show you how to construct the shade itself, though you can also transfer the design to a regular shade for a more simple version.

designer: **CHRIS NOAH-COOPER**

What You Need

- Piece of orange paper for arc, 65- to 80-pound cover weight stock, 6 x 10 x 7¼ inches (15 x 25.5 x 18.5 cm)
- Pencil
- Terry cloth towel
- Needle piercer
- Piece of framing glass
- Craft knife
- Craft glue
- Watercolors and acrylic paint in assorted colors: shades of black, gray, blue, orange, yellow, and white
- Tracing paper, same dimensions as arc (see above)
- 6-inch (15-cm) top lamp shade ring
- 10-inch (25.5-cm) bottom lamp shade ring
- Wooden clothespins
- Small piece of masking tape or paper clip
- Wax paper
- Weights
- ⅝-inch (1.6-cm) grosgrain cotton ribbon trim (or 50/50 cotton/polyester blend), 64 inches (163 cm)

What You Do

Photocopy the pattern on page 66 and transfer the pattern lightly to the back side of the arc with a pencil. You can either use a light table or tape the design and the paper on a window and trace. Prepare a work surface by folding a terry cloth towel in half and placing the arc on top of it with its right side facing down. Use the needle piercer to make the pierced holes in the paper (shown as dotted lines on pattern). (Piercers can be found in larger craft supply stores.)

· · · · · · · ·

Once the piercing is complete, tape the edges of a sheet of framing glass and place the arc with its right side facing down. Begin the cutwork with a craft knife. Any unbroken lines on the pattern can be cut. Cut as much or as little as you wish. Use gentle pressure; beginners often use too much pressure, which breaks off the knife blade. For this reason, wear eye protection. Small tears can be fixed with a small amount of craft glue.

The next step is to go over the design with paint. Use the photograph as a guide. Since this is an essentially monochromatic illustration, it's important to use different shades of dark colors and vary brush strokes; this keeps it from looking flat. Do not use too much water when painting larger landscape areas, as the paper will buckle. When the paint is dry, sculpt the cut areas. Working from the back side, use piercer to work cut edges up. Gently fold the paper up (to the inside) and roll over piercer.

• • • • • • • •

This designer lined the arc with tracing paper for a more finished look, but this step is optional. To line the shade, first run a line of glue across the top of the arc, and put tracing paper down along the top over the arc. Once the tops of the sheets are anchored together, glue from the center to ends until the tracing paper lies flat on the arc. Smooth paper with your hands to prevent bulging. Allow to dry thoroughly, then trim with a craft knife.

• • • • • • • •

Now that you have finished your design, you are ready to construct the shade. Hold the bottom wire ring in line with your body with one hand. Hold the bottom center front of the arc on the wire ring and fasten the edge with a wooden clothespin. Alternating work between the left and the right sides, continue fitting and fastening the arc to the ring, using a generous number of clothespins until you reach the end of the arc.

• • • • • • • •

Return to the center front and fit the right half to the ring. When you reach the end, overlap the back seam, left over right, and fasten with a clothespin. Make sure the arc has no gaps and that the arc's edge fits evenly around the edge. Fit the top ring to the arc in the same manner. Check the top and the bottom for a smooth, snug fit. With the back seam facing you, lightly mark the top and bottom seam allowance. Remove all clothespins and set rings aside. Place the arc on a flat surface with its right side facing up. Connect the top and bottom markings and trim off any excess material. Turn the arc over so its right side faces up. Apply a line of glue along the entire length of both sides of the back seam overlap.

Line up the top right edge of the arc with the left side's pencil mark and fasten with a small piece of masking tape or a paper clip placed perpendicular to the arc's edge. Secure the bottom in the same way. Hold the glued seamlines together with two hands. Place the arc, seam side down, on wax paper and remove the clothespins. Clean off any excess glue with a clean cloth, then place weights along the back seam. Allow to dry for one hour.

• • • • • • • •

Apply glue around the arc's bottom inside edge, then put top frame in and clip with clothespins. Make sure edge of paper is tight on the ring, working with one side of the frame against your body. Glue the top ring in place in the same way. You may need to work with the rings to get them in place properly. Allow glue to dry for one hour.

• • • • • • • •

Next, finish the top and the bottom with ribbon trim. Preshrink the trim by washing it with dishwasher soap in warm water. Allow to dry thoroughly. Working from the back seam, position the binding ¼ inch (.5 cm) to the left of the seam overlap. (The bottom edge of the ribbon should just cover the guide line.) Press the trim into place with your fingers and allow several minutes to dry.

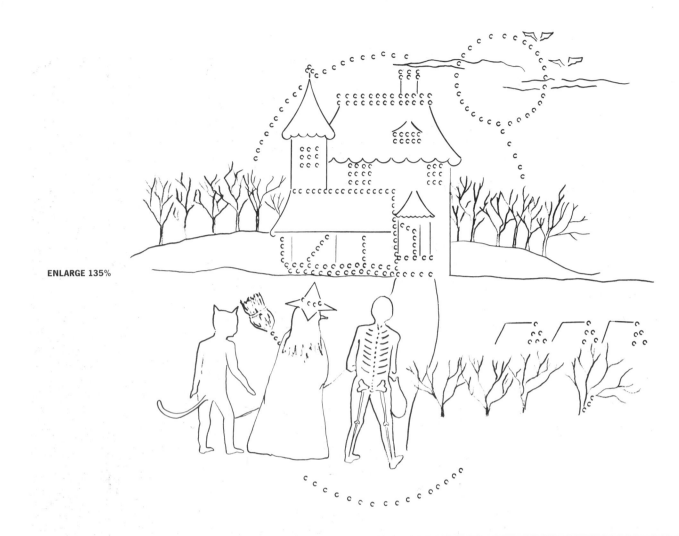

ENLARGE 135%

Trick-or-Treating

THERE is some disagreement about how and when the American custom of "trick-or-treating" began. The custom itself is quite new, but the idea behind it has been around for centuries. It most likely grew, to some degree, from the Celtic practice of leaving food or milk on the steps for roaming spirits for Samhain (see page 12). People began to disguise themselves as spirits and went out begging for treats. If the inhabitants of the house did not supply the treats, the beggers would play a practical joke on the owner of the house.

In addition, it has long been the custom of the poor in Ireland, in particular, to go from house to house, begging for food or money; sometimes they claimed the contributions were for Muck Olla, a Druid god. If the occupants were unwilling to contribute, the beggers would threaten to call down the wrath of the saints.

Ancient Celts also gave cakes to the poor on Samhain, with the single request that the poor pray for a good harvest. The English had a custom of "souling" or going door to door begging for "soul cakes," or sweet, square cakes with currants, on All Souls' Day, or November 2. When the poor received goodies, they promised to pray for dead family members.

Soda Can Votives

Recycle your leftover soda cans and make these adorable votive candle holders. It is a great rainy-day project, since very few materials (and very little time) is required. These holders can also be used as napkin rings for a Halloween dinner party.

What You Need

- 12-ounce (340 g) aluminum soda can
- Craft scissors
- Pencil
- Craft knife
- Paper edger or hole puncher (optional)
- Stapler or duct tape
- Votive candle

designer: **MELANIE WOODSON**

What You Do

Clean and dry soda can thoroughly. Using a sharp pair of craft scissors, cut off the top of the soda can. Be careful: the metal edges may be sharp. Next, cut along seam of aluminum can, and use your palm to press can flat. Wash and dry metal again, if necessary.

Trace or sketch the jack-o'-lantern design onto the clear side of the metal with a pencil, then use the scissors or a craft knife to cut out the inside portions of the design first. (Depending on the design, a paper edger or hole puncher may prove useful.)

Next, carefully cut around the outside of the pumpkin with scissors. Cut a band around the bottom of the can, and shape the band into a circle. Secure band in place with a stapler or duct tape. Make sure the circle is wide enough for votive candle. Position candle inside circle.

Mosaic Pumpkins

*You don't need to be an expert mosaicist to create tile-work hats
for these charming terra-cotta pumpkin lanterns. It's just a matter of
assembling pieces of broken plates—readily available at flea markets
and thrift stores—on a store-bought terra-cotta form. If you're
feeling really creative, try covering the entire pumpkin.*

designer: **TERRY TAYLOR**

What You Need

- 6 or 7 assorted dishes in a variety of colors
- Stained-glass "gems" (optional)
- Terra-cotta pumpkin lantern
- Tile nippers
- Goggles or safety glasses
- Cement mortar
- Small disposable palette knife or disposable picnic knife
- Plastic to cover work surface
- Dry grout
- Disposable rubber/latex gloves and mixing containers
- Grout float or polyethylene foam wrap (white packaging material)

What You Do

Purchase a terra-cotta pumpkin lantern in the desired size at any local garden center (pumpkins available only in fall). Flea markets are excellent sources for plates and decorative elements. When selecting your plates, keep the color theme in mind; be forewarned: orange is not an easy color to find, so start looking long before Halloween.

. . . .

First, assemble your assortment of plates. Beginning at the outer rim and working toward the flat center of each plate, use the tile nippers to cut the plates into irregular pieces. Don't worry about the size of the pieces at this point. **NOTE:** Always wear safety glasses when breaking/nipping plates with your tile nippers! Once you have the edges of the plates removed, make smaller pieces about ½ inch (1.5 cm) in length and width. These pieces will be used on the outer edges of the hat. Set them aside. Take the remaining pieces and make slightly larger squares/rectangles. Set these pieces aside as well. Sort the pieces according to color and contour.

Mix a small batch of cement mortar according to the manufacturer's instructions, allowing it to cure briefly as directed. Working in from the outer edge of the hat, begin to attach the plate pieces. The pieces from the plate rim should be used along the outer edge of the hat. Use a disposable knife to apply a small amount of mortar to each piece, and set it in place. If you wish, apply a row of stained-glass "gems" to the hat.

. . . .

Continue to place pieces around the edge of the hat. Use your nippers to trim pieces to fit if necessary. Fill in the rest of the hat with the remaining flat pieces. Space tiles out with about ⅛ inch (.3 cm) or less between each tile. Allow to dry overnight (or longer) before grouting.

. . . .

Cover your work surface with plastic before grouting. Mix the grout according to the manufacturer's instructions, and apply it to the surface of the hat with a small piece of polyethylene foam wrap or grout float. Use the foam as a spreading tool, and wipe the grout between the spaces of the tiles. Work the grout into the spaces. Allow the grout to set (about 15 minutes), then use the foam to wipe the excess grout from the surface. Continue until the excess grout is removed.

. . . .

After about half an hour, use a barely damp sponge to remove grout haze from the surface. Continue wiping until clean. Allow the grout to dry overnight, and wipe the surface clean again as needed.

. . . .

Use a small tea light or votive candle to illuminate the pumpkin. Do not allow the pumpkin to be subjected to freezing weather or freezing rain.

Skeleton Votive Holder

A colorful gourd carved with eerie skeletons is an unusual alternative to the traditional carved pumpkin—and this gourd will last for many Halloweens to come.

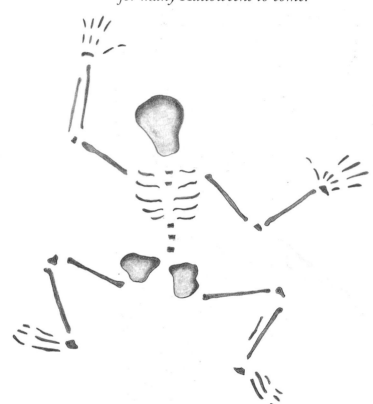

What You Need

- Small basket-type gourd, cured and cleaned
- Pencil
- Skeleton pattern (see left)
- Craft knife
- Wood-burning tool
- Leather dye or watered-down acrylic paint, orange
- Small glass votive holder and candle

What You Do

Cured gourds are widely available year-round at farmers' markets and floral supply stores. Basket-type gourds are one of the most commonly sold gourd shapes.

·······

Use a pencil to sketch a hole in the top of the gourd and cut it out with a craft knife. Clean the inside of all the pulp and seeds. Transfer the skeleton pattern (provided) onto the gourd with a pencil. This gourd has room for three skeletons, though this will vary, depending on the size of the gourd. Working slowly and carefully, use a wood-burning tool or a craft knife to cut out the design.

·······

Paint the gourd with orange leather dye or watered-down acrylic paint, and allow to dry thoroughly. Insert a glass votive candle holder (with candle) inside the gourd.

move over!

In the Middle Ages in Europe, graveyards were so overcrowded that dead bodies were dug up to make room for new ones. For that reason, wealthy people paid to be buried inside churches (sometimes in caskets placed along the church walls) or in graves underneath the church floor. (Inside the church, one was assured a more long-lasting resting spot.)

BELOW: Photograph taken at the home of Pat Lytle (Asheville, NC).

designer: **GINGER SUMMIT**

Jack-o'-Lanterns

BECAUSE of the Irish Potato Famine (1845-50), over 700,000 Irish people immigrated to the United States. These immigrants brought with them traditions of Halloween, including the tradition of the jack-o'-lantern. Though the original jack-o'-lantern was made with a turnip, the Irish immigrants had to use a more readily available replacement—the pumpkin, a fruit that is unique to the Americas. (In some parts of Europe, turnips are still the preferred jack-o'-lantern.)

Legend has it that a stingy Irish blacksmith named Jack crossed paths with the Devil in a pub on Halloween night. Jack was a drunkard, and on this particular night, he had consumed one too many. His judgement was blurred, to be sure, and Jack nearly fell into the hands of the Devil. To save himself, Jack offered to exchange his soul for one last drink at the bar.

BELOW: An assortment of Jack-o'-lanterns arranged on a stairway, carved by Chris Rich (top and bottom left), Sally Krahl (top right), and Nichole Tuggle (bottom right)

The Devil agreed to the exchange and turned himself into a sixpence to pay the bartender. In a quick move, Jack put the sixpence in his purse. The Devil was unable to change himself back, since the purse also held a silver cross. Jack agreed to release the Devil only after the Devil agreed to wait 10 years to claim Jack's soul.

Ten years later to the day, the Devil returned. Jack was walking along a country road when the Devil appeared. Jack said, "I'll go, but before I go, will you get me an apple from that tree?" Seeing nothing unreasonable about the request, the Devil jumped on Jack's shoulders to retrieve the apple. Jack pulled a knife from his pocket and carved a cross in the trunk of the tree. The Devil was thus stranded in the air and unable to retrieve Jack's soul. Jack made the Devil promise to abandon his quest for Jack's soul, and the Devil, seeing no other choice, agreed.

In spite of his cleverness with respect to the Devil, Jack was not admitted to Heaven when he died. It seems he had spent his life as a stingy, deceitful drunkard. Neither was he admitted into Hell—the Devil turned him away, staying true to his promise to never take Jack's soul. As Jack was cast out of Hell, he begged the Devil to at least provide a light to lead Jack through the dark. In a final gesture, the Devil threw a live coal at Jack straight from the fire of Hell. To light his way without allowing the light to be extinguished, Jack placed the coal inside the turnip he was eating.

Ever since, according to the Irish folk tale, Jack has wandered in darkness (awaiting Judgement Day) with his lantern and has become the symbol of the damned soul.

The ancient Celts believed that ghosts and spirits left their graves on Halloween and sought warmth in their former homes. To prevent the ghosts from coming near, people dressed in scary costumes and left treats and goodies on their doorsteps to appease the spirits. It also became the custom to carve a hollowed turnip with a face (or to paint one) and place lighted candles inside to scare any evil spirits away.

designer: **HEATHER SMITH**

Witchy Lamp Shade

*A wicked witch-hat shade
will cast a luminous spell
in any room of your house.*

What You Need

- Metal lathe
- Wire
- Black tissue paper (or any other thin paper)
- Green tissue paper (or any other thin paper)
- Clear-drying wood glue
- Spray adhesive
- Needle-nose pliers
- Wire cutters

quick candle holder

Cut a hole in the top of a miniature pumpkin or a small ornamental gourd. Spoon the seeds out of the pumpkin or squash, then press a candle into the hole.

What You Do

First, you will need to choose the lamp your shade will rest on. Decide how large your finished shade will be at its base, then cut the metal lathe to that size. (Be sure the shade is wide enough to leave room around the bulb for ventilation.) Since the shade is cone shaped, cut away the upper right and left corners of the metal. Set leftover pieces aside for later.

. . . .

Begin shaping the metal by hand to form a cone shape, with the narrowest section of the cone at the top. Secure the shade by using pliers to clamp and crush the metal together wherever the layers meet. For additional strength, weave wire through both layers along the seam. Bend the tip of the cone, but do not flatten it; you should leave room for rising heat to pass through.

. . . .

At the base of the cone, begin bending the metal upward to form the brim of the hat. It will be necessary for you to make three or four cuts along the edge so that the metal will spread out. Fill the gaps by attaching leftover pieces of lathe, and secure with wire or by pinching the edges together.

. . . .

Check the finished lamp shade framework against the chosen lamp and make adjustments as needed. If necessary, attach a piece of wire inside the top of the hat so the shade will rest on the light bulb more securely.

. . . .

Draw a witch shape on a square piece of black tissue paper and carefully cut it out; a stencil works well if you do not feel comfortable freehanding the design. Cut a square of green paper to fit behind the space, and glue these two pieces together. (You should then have a green witch framed by black paper.) Make as many witches as desired to space around the hat. You may choose to use other Halloween motifs, as well, and alternate them with the witch.

In a well-ventilated area, spray adhesive onto the entire hat frame. Place the witch cutouts around the hat and press to secure in place. Wrap the rest of the framework in one layer of black tissue paper. Use any remaining green paper to cover the underside of the brim. Be careful how far you layer inside the hat, because the paper may scorch if it is too close to the bulb.

. . . .

Gently brush wood glue over the first layer of paper, and before this dries, wrap the shade in a second layer. Do not put another layer over the witch cutouts, because this is where most of the light will pass through. Coat entire shade again in wood glue, and allow to dry thoroughly. This coating of wood glue helps the paper shrink to the frame, and will also harden for durability.

Witch-Hunts

MOST PEOPLE THINK of a witch as an old, ugly woman dressed in flowing black with a crooked nose and a broom as her primary mode of transportation. Today, partly because a witch outfit is a favorite Halloween costume, the witch has taken on a harmless and almost humorous persona, with exaggerated features and a black, pointed hat.

There was a time when most people believed that witches were followers of Satan and lived clandestinely among us. Illness, death, and accidents were frequently blamed on the magic spells of witches. The word witch comes from *wicce*, an Old English word meaning "one who practices magic." In ancient Egypt and the early Roman Empire, the practice of witchcraft was commonplace; followers destroyed crops, vandalized religious objects and churches, and even exhumed dead bodies.

Until the beginning of the 13th century, Church leaders taught that witchcraft was a superstition and that witches had no real power. But sometime in the same century, the Church decided that witches were, in fact, worshipers of the Devil with special powers. At this point, Church members waged a war on witchcraft and the great witch-hunts

of Europe thus began. Anyone could bring charges of witchcraft against whomever they pleased. Sometimes people were accused out of pure spite. Accused witches were tortured horribly until they confessed. Perhaps not surprisingly, a confession was almost always forthcoming. The last witch was burned in Europe in 1782.

The summer of 1692 in Salem, Massachusetts, was one of history's most famous witch-hunts. It began when a group of girls accused a black woman named Tituba of causing them to go into fits. Nineteen Salem citizens were subsequently accused of witchcraft and hanged. (A dog was also executed.)

Puritans in New England became terrified of witches. Women were accused of changing themselves into animals and causing any number of evil events to occur. The accusations flew out of control, and women were accused of witchery based on the most bizarre (and unsubstantiated) evidence. One woman was accused because someone claimed that only a witch could get an apple inside a dumpling the way she did. Luckily, the woman had the good sense to demonstrate her technique in court and was acquitted.

designer: **GINGER SUMMIT**

Gourd String Lights

A string of colorful ghosts and jack-o'-lanterns makes a playful adornment for a porch railing or entryway. Ornamental gourds have a thin shell that is easily cut with a craft knife or a wood-burning tool. For this project, you will need miniature gourds that are about 2 to 4 inches (5 to 10 cm) in diameter.

What You Need

- Miniature round ornamental gourds, cured and cleaned (for the pumpkin lights)
- Miniature bottle-shaped ornamental gourds, cured and cleaned (for the ghost lights)
- Pencil
- Craft knife or wood-burning tool
- Leather dye or watered-down acrylic paint, white and orange
- String of lights
- Cardboard or plastic
- Floral tape or craft clay

What You Do

Cured gourds are widely available year-round at farmers' markets and floral supply stores. Ornamental gourds are among the most common gourd varieties.

∙∙∙∙∙∙∙

Draw a jagged line (see photograph) around the bottom of each gourd and carefully cut bottom out with a craft knife or a wood-burning tool. Drill a hole in the top of the gourd large enough for the light bulb.

∙∙∙∙∙∙∙

Soak the bottle-shaped gourds (to be used for the ghosts) in water for 15 minutes, then use a craft knife or a wood-burning tool to cut two armlike slits in each gourd. Use your fingers to gently pull the arms away from the body of the gourd, and wedge toothpicks between the arms and body. Allow to dry with toothpicks in place, then remove toothpicks.

∙∙∙∙∙∙∙

Sketch eyes and mouth on the ghost gourds, and use the craft knife or a wood-burning tool to cut these out. (A wood-burning tool works better for detail work.)

Sketch jack-o'-lantern faces on the pumpkin gourds, and use the craft knife or a wood-burning tool to cut design out.

∙∙∙∙∙∙∙

Paint the ghost gourds with white leather dye or watered-down acrylic paint, and allow to dry thoroughly. Paint the pumpkin gourds with orange leather dye or watered-down acrylic paint, and allow to dry thoroughly.

∙∙∙∙∙∙∙

For these lights, the designer purchased a string of colored lights, and inserted orange lights into each socket; white string lights also work, but tend to be less colorful. To secure the gourd to the light: Cut one small doughnut-shaped washer out of cardboard or plastic for each gourd. Remove the light bulb from the socket, and gently push the cardboard washer over the threaded end of the bulb; and with the light bulb and cardboard washer on the inside of the gourd, screw the bulb back into the socket. Use floral tape or craft clay on the outside of the gourd to hold the socket in the correct position.

The Ghosts of Borley Rectory

ENGLAND'S BORLEY RECTORY is one of the world's most famous haunted houses. The property, which was originally a Benedictine monastery, eventually passed to the Waldegrave family, who occupied it for three decades. The rectory itself was built in 1863 by Reverend Henry Bull, a descendant of the Waldegraves. For reasons that are still unclear, strange happenings began to occur after Borley Rectory was constructed.

Legend has it that a nun fell in love with a monk, and the two tried unsuccessfully to elope. The unlucky couple, it seems, were intercepted on their way out of the monastery—they had almost escaped in a horse and carriage. For their deception, the two were severely punished. The monk was hanged, and the nun was walled up alive in the rectory walls. The nun is among the ghosts said to haunt the rectory to this day, and numerous people claim to have heard or seen visions of the ill-fated horse

and carriage. Henry Bull himself is also believed to have haunted the rectory; he has been spotted wearing the gray jacket in which he died at Borley.

In the 1920s, the house was purchased by Lionel Foyster and his wife, Marianne; they moved into Borley Rectory October 16, 1930, and recorded more than 2,000 paranormal events in their five-year stay there, including strange sounds, events, and mysterious writings on the walls. Supposedly, a ghost locked Marianne in her bedroom and even threw her out of bed.

In 1936, Borley Rectory burned down. Some believe the ghosts moved across the street to Borley Church; others contend they still roam the site. In 1945, what was thought to be the remains of the unfortunate nun were found—and she was finally given a proper burial. Nonetheless, the legend of Borley lives on, and visitors still go to the site in search of its ghosts.

watch that candle

An old European
superstition held that if
a candle flame turned blue,
it was an indication
that a ghost was
in the house!

Halloween Cookie-Cutter Candles

*Using cookie cutters with Halloween motifs to create designs
in wax is a great way to turn traditional molded candles
into spooky Halloween mood lighting.*

designer: **PAMELA BROWN**

What You Need

- 2 to 3 pounds (908 to 1,362 g) paraffin wax with a 135° to 145° F (57° to 63° C) melting point (exact amount depends on size of mold)
- Candle dye, orange and black (cut into slivers)
- 3 to 4 ounces (85 to 113 g) stearic acid (use one part stearic acid per 10 parts wax)
- 1 to 2 feet (.3 to .6 m) of 4- to 5-inch (10- to 12.5-cm) candle wick (use size appropriate for individual candle mold)
- Double-boiler setup
- Candy thermometer
- Ladle
- Baking sheet or pie plate
- Cookie cutters with Halloween motifs
- Vegetable spray
- Mold seal
- Wick support (can use chopstick or length of sturdy wire)
- Pyramid candle mold
- Skillet or griddle (optional)

What You Do

Melt a small amount of wax (approximately 10 ounces or 284 g) in the double boiler. Clip a candy thermometer to the side of the pan, and allow the wax to heat until a temperature of about 180° F (82° C) is achieved. NOTE: Do not leave the pot unattended for any reason while the hot wax is melting. It is very important that the wax not get too hot. The flash point (point at which the wax will ignite) varies for different types of wax; make sure you know what it is for your wax before you begin.

········

Add several shavings of dye to the wax in the color you wish to make the cut-out shapes. Check the color and add more dye as needed. When the dye is completely melted, and the desired color is achieved, use a ladle to pour wax onto baking sheet or pie plate to a thickness of about 1/3 inch (.8 cm). Allow wax to cool until still soft, but not liquid. Press cookie cutters into wax to create cutouts. Remove shapes from pan and allow to cool and harden. One caution: Make sure the cookie cutters you choose are not wider than the sides of the candle mold.

Melt remaining wax to same temperature as before and add stearic acid. Prime the wick by dipping it in the melted wax once. Add dye slivers of the color you wish to be the primary candle color to the wax until desired color is achieved.

········

Spray the inside of the pyramid mold with vegetable spray. Thread primed wick through the hole at the end of the mold, leaving 1/2 inch (1.5 cm) outside of the hole. Cover hole with mold seal. Invert the pyramid into its holder (or other metal container that will allow it to sit balanced and secure). Tie the other end of the wick to the wick support until taut, and place wire or stick across the width of the mold. NOTE: Many pyramid candle molds come with a mold holder/balance and a wick support. If yours does not, any metal container that will allow the mold to sit balanced and secure will work for the holder; use a chopstick or length of wire for the wick support.

········

Pour the melted wax into the pyramid mold until the mold is about half full. Immediately place Halloween cutouts inside mold, upside-down with flat surfaces against the sides of the mold. In order to make the cutouts stick, place at least halfway down into wax first to form a glue to help them stay in place against the sides of the mold. When the cut-outs are in place, ladle more wax into mold until mold is full.

········

Let the wax cool. As the wax cools, it will shrink, and air pockets will form. You will need to prick the surface of the candle occasionally with a piece of wire, then top off the candle with additional wax. Allow candle to sit overnight or in the refrigerator until completely cool. Remove the mold seal and untie the wick support. Remove candle from mold. (You may need to rap the mold on a hard surface to help release the candle.) Trim the wick.

········

TIP: To remove any film or unevenness on surface of candle, place candle on hot skillet or griddle, and slide the candle back and forth on each side for a few seconds until surface is smooth.

eerie edibles

dry ice safety alert

Though dry ice is a fabulous addition to any Halloween party table, it should never be consumed. Don't put it directly in your punch and never touch it with bare hands. To make dry ice steam, pour hot water over it (in a container) and stir with a spoon. Dry ice will last up to eight hours in the refrigerator, but will only steam for about five minutes after water is added.

Spicy Witch's Brew

This brew is a delicious Halloween punch; the apple cider and cinnamon give it a crisp, autumnal flavor. For added witchy effect, purchase blocks of dry ice and place them under (or behind) the punch bowl; dry ice is inexpensive and can be had from ice suppliers.

What You Need

- 1 12-ounce (340 g) can frozen orange juice concentrate
- ¼ cup (60 ml) lemon juice
- 2 quarts (2 l) apple cider
- 4 cups (960 ml) water
- 1 cup (240 ml) white grape juice
- 1½ teaspoons ground cinnamon
- 1 package (.13 ounce or 3.65 g) cherry soft drink mix (for ice)
- Large bowl
- Ice trays (approximately three)

What You Do

Mix the orange juice, lemon juice, apple cider, water, white grape juice, and ground cinnamon together in a large bowl until well blended. Chill for at least an hour in the refrigerator before serving.

••••••••

Make a pitcher of cherry soft drink and pour into ice trays. When frozen, add to the witch's brew to look like bloody ice.

designer: **CHRIS BRYANT**

decorating with dead blooms

Gather dried, browned, and dead flowers and leaves for Halloween party decorations.
Usually dead foliage is available in your backyard or on the side of the road, but for
high-quality dead material, contact your local florist.

Pumpkin and Ghost Soup

Here's a Halloween version of a savory traditional bean soup. The concept is simple: make a delectable black bean soup, then garnish it with sliced carrots (pumpkins) and whole hard-boiled eggs (ghosts). We've provided two methods: a slow-cook method and a quicker version using canned beans.

What You Need

for soup:

- 2 cups (378 g) dried (or four 15-ounce (425-g) cans black beans)
- 2 quarts (1 l) water for soaking beans and 2 quarts (1 l) fresh water for soup (or four 15-ounce (425-g) cans chicken broth)
- 1–2 large onions, diced
- 1 rib celery, diced
- 1–2 carrots, diced
- Ham, ham bone, or any other seasoning meat
- 2 cloves garlic
- 1 teaspoon salt
- 2 teaspoons sugar
- ½ teaspoon black pepper

for garnish:

- 5–7 carrots, cut into ½-inch (1.5-cm) slices
- 6 small eggs

What You Do

Pick over beans, add 2 quarts (1 l) water, and soak overnight. Drain and rinse thoroughly. If you do not have time to soak the beans, rapidly bring the beans to a boil, boil for two minutes, then immediately remove from heat. Soak beans for one hour, then drain and rinse.

Add 2 quarts (1 l) fresh water to the beans, then stir in the onions, celery, carrots, meat seasoning, garlic, salt, sugar, and black pepper. Simmer for two hours or cook in a crock pot (High: 5–6 hours. Low: 10–12 hours). Remove from heat and puree until desired texture is achieved. Adjust seasoning and add more liquid if soup is too thick. Keep warm while you prepare seasoning.

A shortcut: If you do not have time to slow-cook this soup, you can use four 15-ounce (425-g) cans of black beans and four 15-ounce (425-g) cans of chicken broth with the same seasonings. You may need to add water if the soup is too thick.

For the garnish, place carrots (five to seven medium) and eggs in a saucepan, cover with water, and bring to a boil. Cook until eggs are hard-boiled, or about 10 to 15 minutes, then drain. (Depending on the size, the carrots may need to boil up to 10 minutes more.) Peel eggs. Just before serving, stir carrots into soup. Place one egg into each bowl, then ladle soup over eggs. Serve with salad and crusty bread. Makes 6 servings

designer: **TERRY BREWER**

Haunted House Cake

Although experts on well-built structures may cringe at the idea,
this haunted house is completely edible. Scan the isles of your local
supermarket for foods that provide even more ghostly touches.

What You Need

- 2 boxes chocolate cake mix
- Square of cardboard
- 2 16-ounce (453-g) containers milk chocolate frosting (amount may vary)
- 10 graham crackers (amount may vary)
- 5 Vienna wafers (amount may vary)
- 10 sugar wafers (amount may vary)
- 5 round butter cookies (amount may vary)
- ½ pound (227 g) confectioners' sugar
- 1 egg white
- Food color paste: yellow and black
- 2 loaf pans
- Knife
- Pastry bag
- 2 jelly beans (one black and one orange)
- 1 licorice stick

What You Do

First, bake two chocolate cakes in separate loaf pans. Allow both cakes to cool thoroughly before constructing the house. Trim one cake square with a knife, and save the scrap cake pieces and crumbs. The other cake will need to remain rounded, as the rounded top will serve as the roof. Stack the rounded cake on top of the square one, and center the cakes on top of a piece of sturdy cardboard. Use the scrap pieces of cake to make the turret and the steps; attach to the main house with a layer of chocolate frosting.

Cover the entire house, roof, turret, and cardboard with a layer of milk chocolate frosting. Use a knife to make lines in the frosting for a more realistic effect. Sprinkle leftover cake crumbs on the cardboard for dirt. Break graham crackers into pieces for the shingles and attach to roof in layers; use additional frosting, if necessary, to secure shingles. Do the same with the turret's roof.

Gently insert an entire graham cracker into the front part of the house for an awning, and press a Vienna wafer to the front section for the doorway; you will probably need to add a layer of frosting to the back of the wafer first. The windows are made with sugar wafers. The designer found that when the wafers are pulled apart, the direction of the design can be used to represent different parts of the house. The windows have wafers with a diagonal grid, and the shutters use an up-and-down grid.

Place a round butter cookie above the doorway and sections of butter cookies above each window. Create a graveyard by pressing Vienna wafers into the frosting on the cardboard (you may need to add more frosting) at different angles and heights.

Next, you will need to create what is called "royal icing" by beating together an egg white and the confectioners' sugar; this creates a fairly stiff frosting that dries hard like candy. The bats and ghosts are made of this frosting, as well as the yellow window covering. After you have beaten the egg and sugar together, separate the frosting into three parts: add yellow food color paste to one section, black paste to the second section, and leave the third section white.

Use a knife to spread the yellow icing on the windows for a spooky, stained-glass effect. Use a pastry bag to make the ghosts (in the graveyard, entryway, and window); cut small pieces of orange and black jelly beans for the eyes and mouth. Make the bats with a pastry bag as well, placing them wherever it seems appropriate. Create a pane in the sugar wafer above the doorway with black icing.

Make cuts in the licorice stick for a tree and attach to the cardboard with chocolate frosting. You may need to lean it against the house somewhat for stability.

The Black Hound

toasting pumpkin seeds

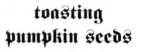

This delicious snack is made
from pumpkin seeds gleaned from the
Halloween jack-o'-lantern. First, separate
the seeds from the pumpkin pulp (a messy
job, but fittingly slimy). Place the pumpkin
seeds in a bowl of water and scoop seeds
into a colander. Wash the seeds thoroughly
and spread on a cookie sheet that has
been lined with wax paper. Drizzle seeds
with vegetable oil and sprinkle with
coarse salt. Place in the oven on 250°F
(120°C) for approximately one hour
or until slightly brown.

LONG AGO IN A SMALL VILLAGE in England, the townspeople had the custom of burying a dog alive under the cornerstone of a new church, in order to protect the church from witches. The dog's ghost, they presumed, would remain to keep watch over the churchyard and drive away any unwanted spirits.

One night, shortly after a new church had been built, the village pastor left his small house, which was located behind the church, to visit a family whose young son was very sick. He grabbed his walking stick in one hand and pulled his warm cloak around him with the other, shielding himself from the bitter winds that were howling across the moors.

The pastor set out down the narrow dirt path that led toward the churchyard gate, which opened onto the lane. As he bustled along the path, thinking of how the treetops looked eerily like spindly fingers straining to grab hold of the white, round moon rising behind them, his ears detected a sound. "Pit-pat-pit-pat-pit-pat." Was it coming from behind him or in front of him? He couldn't tell, so he walked on.

Again he heard "pit-pat-pit-pat-pit-pat." The sound grew louder, but he saw nothing ahead of him on the path. He stopped abruptly, turned around, and peered through the dark night. Yet, his eyes could make out no shape to accompany the sound that was coming closer and closer to him in the darkness. Terrified, he pulled his cloak more tightly around his shoulders and hurried for the churchyard gate.

Before he could reach the tall iron gate, however, an icy chill blast through the pastor's body. It was much colder than any winter wind he had ever encountered, and he felt as if he had on no cloak at all, as his arms and legs froze, and his heart nearly stopped beating from the cold.

The pastor was paralyzed by the frigid spell; only his eyes could move, and they grew wide in horror at what he saw next.

Two enormous black paws with sharp curved claws emerged out of the pastor's body, then two strong black legs, then a huge, horrible black head with snarling lips that hid a set of gleaming, wet fangs. The pastor was nearly dead of fright when he realized what had happened. The ghost of the watchdog was passing through him as it tore around the churchyard on its nightly rounds. His own body was not hurt, and the cold spell left as suddenly as it had come.

In spite of his sheer terror, the pastor congratulated himself on burying the live dog under the cornerstone to protect the church from evil spirits. Obviously, it was working, he thought, as he stood, waiting to recover his senses. After he had calmed down and was able to breathe again, he raised his head to resume his journey. Immediately, the cold burst of fear rushed back into his body; standing ahead of him in the path, blocking his way, was the horrible ghost of the black hound, snarling and snapping at him.

The pastor tried to call out for help, but his voice was so weak from fright that he hardly made a sound at all. He dropped his walking stick and began to run frantically for his front door, his cloak flying from his shoulders as he raced back up the path. This time, however, instead of a soft "pit-pat-pit-pat-pit-pat," the pastor heard the heavy breathing of the snarling hound on his heels.

The black hound chased the pastor to the cornerstone of the church and stood growling at him, baring fierce, sharp fangs, until the pastor promised to dig up the dog's bones and bury them in the graveyard with the rest of the dead. And thus the ghost of the black hound was put to rest.

more edible hands

Place candy corn in the fingers of baker's gloves and stuff the gloves with popcorn for a yummy Halloween treat.

Creepy (and Crispy) Body Parts

Who says food can't be disgusting and delicious? A variation is to fill a plastic mask and nonpowdered glove with gelatin for extra-jiggly body parts.

designer: **TAMARA MILLER**

What You Need

6 cups (168 g) crispy rice cereal

3 tablespoons (45 g) butter

1 package (10 ounces or about 40) regular marshmallows or 4 cups (184 g) miniature marshmallows

Jelly beans or other colored candy

Red licorice yarn

Plastic mask

Masking tape

Large saucepan

Vegetable spray

Nonpowdered disposable glove

Scissors

What You Do

The first step is to make the crispy rice cereal mixture. In a large pan, melt butter over low heat. Once butter is completely melted, stir in marshmallows until completely melted. Remove mixture from heat, then add crispy rice cereal and stir until cereal is completely coated. **NOTE:** this designer used Halloween-themed crispy rice cereal, which has green and orange pieces.

· · · · · · · ·

Spray hands with vegetable spray. To make the face, tape mouth and eyes (or any other holes) closed on a clean mask, and spray inside of mask thoroughly with vegetable spray. Press rice cereal mixture into mask and allow to set up. Use jelly beans or candy for the eyes and red licorice yarn for the mouth.

· · · · · · · ·

To make monster hand, spray the inside of a nonpowdered disposable glove thoroughly with vegetable spray. Press rice cereal mixture into glove. You will need to work quickly, so the mixture does not harden. When mixture has set up, cut glove away with scissors. Rice cereal mixture should hold its shape. Place hand and face on platter and enjoy!

Frightening Foods

Place food items in buckets, cover the tops of the buckets with artificial cobwebs, and ask folks at your haunted house to plunge their hands into the goo, and guess what they feel. Coat all of these lightly with vegetable oil for an extra-slimy sensation.

BRAINS
Spaghetti squash or wide noodles

FINGERS
Small, rounded carrots drizzled with olive oil

HEARTS
Congeal gelatin in a rectangular cake pan, turn out onto a piece of wax paper, cut piece in half, and use a sharp knife to carve gelatin into a roughly anatomically correct human heart.

EYEBALLS
Peeled grapes, small boiled eggs, or pimento-stuffed olives

FINGERNAILS
Pumpkin seeds or candy corn (with the sharp tips cut off)

SLIME
Pumpkin pulp

WORMS
Jelly worms, pasta (bucatini is particularly wormy)

KIDNEYS
Peeled orange sections

ORGANS
Add flour to peanut butter to make a thick paste, and shape the dough into organ of your choice.

BONES
Rawhide bones (from pet stores) well-coated with vegetable oil

OTHER DISGUSTING (albeit unidentifiable) OPTIONS
Gelatin squares, custard or pudding cubes, mashed bananas, peeled cucumbers, and cottage cheese

Devilishly Delicious Sugar Cookies

This recipe is quick and foolproof—and the results are scrumptious! These make adorable Halloween treats when decorated with black and white icing.

What You Need

1 cup (2 sticks or 230 g) butter, softened
1 cup (200 g) granulated sugar
1 large egg
1 teaspoon vanilla extract
2 teaspoons baking powder
3 cups (375 g) flour
   Decorative icing, white and black
   Large mixing bowl
   Electric beater
   Rolling pin
   Cookie cutters
   Cookie sheet
   Spatula
   Knife

designer: **CORKY KURZMANN**

What You Do

Preheat oven to 400° F (200° C). In a large mixing bowl, cream butter and sugar together until well blended. Gradually beat in egg and vanilla extract. Add baking powder and flour, a cupful at a time, mixing well after every addition. The dough will become very stiff. (Do not chill dough.)

•••••

Separate the dough into two halves and roll each half into a ball. On a floured surface, use a rolling pin to flatten each ball out until it is approximately ⅛ inch (.3 cm) thick. Cut Halloween shapes with cookie cutters; coat cookie cutters in flour before each use. Bake on an ungreased cookie sheet for approximately seven minutes or until cookies have a light brown surface. Allow cookies to cool thoroughly.

•••••

To make ghosts, spoon white icing onto center of cookie and spread with a spatula. Make ghost eyes with dots of black icing. To make spider webbing, spread white icing on cookie, then (while the icing is still wet) pipe a spiral of black icing on the cookie, working from the center to the outer edge. Drag a knife from the center of the spiral to the outer edges of the cookie to create webbing. The same technique is used for the bats, except black is used for the base color, and white is piped on in lines to form webbing.

Peanut Butter Pumpkins

Make these quick, bite-sized pumpkins for a last-minute Halloween get-together. You can also add jack-o'-lantern faces with a tube of black icing.

What You Need

1 stick (115 g) butter

1 small jar (12 ounces or 340 g) peanut butter

1 box (16 ounces or 453 g) confectioners' sugar, sifted

Red and yellow food coloring, several drops each

Tube of green icing

Large bowl

Wooden spoon

Toothpick

What You Do

Melt butter in a large bowl and add drops of red and yellow food coloring until the butter has a nice orange color. Add peanut butter and confectioners' sugar, and use a wooden spoon to mix everything together thoroughly until a doughlike consistency is achieved.

• • • • •

Shape dough into small balls. Make ridges on the pumpkins with a toothpick. Add a small amount of green icing to the top of each pumpkin for a stem. Makes 15 to 20 pumpkins, depending on size.

designer: **TAMARA MILLER**

The Pumpkin Man

ZACK WHITESIDE beams with pride as he gazes around his home in Lake Lure, North Carolina, and surveys his pumpkins. It's the first week in October—peak pumpkin time—and there are piles of pumpkins everywhere, all recently harvested from Zack's 20-acre farm. "My father grew pumpkins before me and his father before him," Zack says. "They call me 'The Pumpkin Man'."

Zack has been growing pumpkins since 1950. He and his wife, Del, live in the home that was built by Zack's ancestors around 1760. It's an imposing, yet unpretentious white wooden home—an inviting structure amidst the pumpkins. Zack is a college-educated farmer, and has dabbled in real estate and antiques; Del worked in town for many years. But the two are content to be growing pumpkins full-time now, and devote six months of their year to the business. "Things are much different than when my father grew pumpkins. He was a mule farmer and had 1,000 acres. When I started farming with a tractor, he didn't know what to think."

In the fall, The Pumpkin Center is open to the public pretty much all the time. "If a man wants to buy a punkin," Zack says with a wide grin, "We'll be here to sell him one."

Del cheerfully distributes a self-published cookbook (featuring recipes that use pumpkin, of course) to visitors and friends. Here's a delicious recipe from her collection.

Del's Pumpkin Cookies

What You Need

1½ cups (366 g) pumpkin pulp
or canned pumpkin

½ cup (115 g) butter

1 cup (200 g) granulated sugar

½ teaspoon vanilla

1 cup (100 g) chopped walnuts

1 egg

2 cups (250 g) unsifted flour

1 teaspoon baking powder

1 teaspoon cinnamon

1 20-ounce (567-g) package
butterscotch morsels

What You Do

Mix all the ingredients
in the order given. Drop
by the spoonful onto a
buttered cookie sheet.
Bake in 375° F (190° C)
oven for 12 to 14 minutes.

designer: **CORKY KURZMANN**

Graveyard Pudding

A graveyard topping can also be used with a plain chocolate sheet cake, though chocolate pudding makes for an especially gooey graveyard. The addition of gummy worms (embedded in the cookie-crumb "soil") will surely startle even the hungriest ghoul.

What You Need

3½ cups (840 ml) cold milk

8 ounces (227 g) chocolate instant pudding mix

1 package (16 ounces or 454 g) chocolate sandwich cookies, crushed

5–10 oval-shaped vanilla sandwich cookies

1 tube chocolate decorator icing

1 can whipped cream

Miniature chocolate chips, 2 per ghost

Candy pumpkins

Large mixing bowl

Whisk

Baking pan, 13 x 9 inches (33 x 23 cm)

What You Do

Pour cold milk into large bowl; add pudding mix and stir together. Beat with a wire whisk for several minutes. Stir in half of the crushed cookies. Spoon pudding mixture into the baking pan. Sprinkle pudding with the rest of the crushed chocolate cookies. Refrigerate for one hour or until ready to serve.

• • • • •

Just before you are ready to serve the pudding, use the icing to decorate several of the vanilla sandwich cookies with tombstone messages, and stick cookies into pudding. Make ghosts with a can of whipping cream and position miniature chocolate chips in whipping cream for eyes. Randomly place candy pumpkins around graveyard.

Top Ten Excuses for What Happened to the Candy (to Tell the Kids)

1. The dog ate it.

2. It was contaminated and had to be destroyed. You saved their lives.

3. A Halloween spirit possessed your body and forced you to eat it.

4. It was confiscated by the friendly ghost inhabiting the attic, who was worried about cavities and stomachaches.

5. It vanished. Another unsolved Halloween mystery.

6. One of the trick-or-treaters was a witch, who cast a spell on the family candy; it turned into green slime at midnight on Halloween.

7. The family candy supply was gone, and it had to be given to trick-or-treaters. "Next year, we'll plan better."

8. You gave it away to less-fortunate children.

9. You traded it in for healthy treats; offer them a carrot stick.

10. "That's strange. I have no idea what happened to it." (Practice straight face in advance.)

The Bell Witch

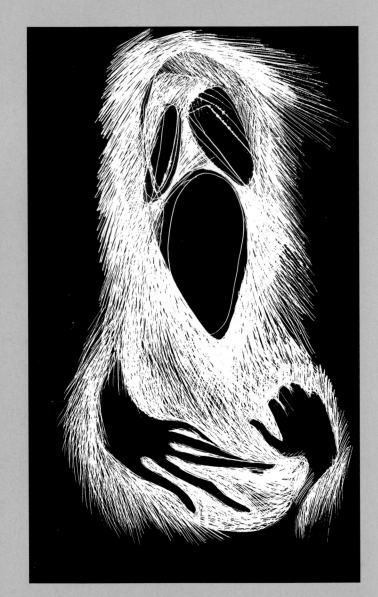

ALONG A ROAD in Tennessee stands the only state sign that commemorates a witch. The sign testifies to the widespread notoriety of the Bell Witch, who spent decades torturing the Bell family of Robertson County and haunting their lands.

Although stories of the Bell Witch vary, the most common tale involves a man named John Bell from North Carolina and a mean-spirited widow named Kate Batts, who lived nearby. After Kate's husband passed away, John helped her settle her estate, and occasionally stopped by to help with chores on her land. Soon John proposed to the widow, unaware of her wicked nature. Once he realized the truly mean spirit of the woman to whom he had pledged himself, however, John wished he could take back his offer of marriage; but he was afraid of what the spiteful woman might do.

One day, while John was helping her repair a shed on her land, the widow stopped to drink from her well, and the heavy bucket hit her in the head, knocking her unconscious. John seized this opportunity to escape his dreadful engagement. He took Kate back to his house, locked her unconscious body in the root cellar, and left her there. Even when she awoke, and he heard her weak pleas for food and water, John did not venture down into the cellar, but allowed his fiancée to perish underground. When he was sure she was finally dead, he retrieved her body from the cellar and carried it back to her well, positioning her on the ground for someone else to discover.

Not long after this trauma, John Bell met a kind woman named Lucy Williams, with whom he fell in love and soon married. The couple moved to Tennessee to start their new life on a farm on the banks of the Red River in 1804, planning for many happy and peaceful years together.

One hot day in 1817, while plowing his fields, John Bell looked up to see an enormous black crow glaring at him from a fence post. The creature stood its ground as he moved toward it, and finally flew at him in attack, flapping its huge wings and threatening to shred him with its sharp claws. A few days later, a similar experience occurred, except this time the creature was a large, snarling animal much like a dog. When Bell shot at it with his shotgun, it disappeared before his eyes. The Bell children also spotted odd creatures in the forests around the farm, and sometimes saw a mysterious old woman wandering in the apple orchard.

Soon, the family began having eerie experiences inside the house. They often heard strange sounds, such as scratching, knocking, and smacking. The sound of a rat gnawing at the bedpost began in the bedroom of the Bells' three sons, and soon spread throughout the house, choosing a new room each night.

The witch did not stop at making sounds, and before long an invisible force began pulling and twisting the hair of the Bell children at night, sending them screaming from their beds in pain and fright. The witch also yanked the sheets off beds at night, and even smacked daughter Betsy Bell in the face on one occasion.

Word of the Bell Witch spread, and people from all over Tennessee began arriving to see, hear, and interact with the spirit. Eventually, the invisible force began to speak, and revealed in a harsh voice her passionate hatred for John Bell, whom she vowed to kill.

According to some stories, the witch of Kate Batts also had a friendly side. Although she tortured John and Betsy Bell and sometimes flogged the Bell slaves, she sang to Mrs. Bell and helped her with chores during an illness. The Bell Witch also supposedly preached to the Bells and others in the community.

Apparently, however, her evil nature won out. Finally, in 1820, the Bell Witch fulfilled her vow to avenge her murder. After afflicting John Bell for some time with a swollen tongue disorder that made it difficult for him to swallow, talk, and even breathe, the witch increased the severity of his affliction. The witch even went so far as to knock the shoes off his feet and throw him to the ground as he tried to walk around the yard in his last days. After a particularly severe beating by the witch, John's doctor sent him to bed with a bottle of medicine. That night, John Bell suffered a violent fit of convulsions and died the next day.

The witch confessed to the murder, laughing gleefully as she told the family that she had exchanged the doctor's prescription with her own dark vial of liquid, a mixture that the doctor proclaimed unidentifiable. The Bell Witch told the family she was leaving the following year, but would return in seven years. She fulfilled this promise as faithfully as she had the first, bringing the old knocking and gnawing sounds and yanked bed sheets with her. The witch did not stay long, however, claiming upon her departure that she would be back in 107 years.

Bell family descendants and other owners of the Bell farm claim they have indeed felt, heard, and seen the witch's presence in the old house, as well as in a cave near the Bell home, where some report hearing heavy chains being dragged along the ground. However, most believe that her days of torturing others have ended. They hope that her revenge on John Bell was enough to keep her evil nature satisfied forever.

Pumpkin-Walnut Muffins

Turn the pumpkin leftover from your jack-o'-lantern into a healthy treat. These muffins are delicious when served with spiced butter at an autumn brunch. The ultimate fall comfort food!

What You Need

- 1 cup (244 g) pumpkin pulp or canned pumpkin
- ½ cup (70 g) packed brown sugar
- ¼ cup (60 g) unsalted butter, melted
- 2 eggs
- 1 cup (125 g) all-purpose flour
- 1 cup (120 g) whole wheat flour
- ½ teaspoon cinnamon
- 2 teaspoons baking powder
- Dash of salt
- ½ cup (50 g) walnuts
- Large mixing bowl
- Small mixing bowl
- Sifter
- Paper muffin liners
- Muffin tin

What You Do

Line a 12-cup muffin pan with paper muffin liners, and preheat the oven to 375° F (190° C). Combine the pumpkin, brown sugar, melted butter, and eggs in a large mixing bowl, and blend the ingredients together thoroughly. Sift the flour (all-purpose and whole wheat) with the cinnamon, baking powder, and salt in a separate bowl.

Gradually add the flour mixture to the pumpkin mixture and blend until just combined, then stir in the walnuts. Spoon the mixture into the already prepared muffin pan. Bake for 20 minutes. Makes 12 muffins.

Spider Treats

Yummy spider treats are especially impressive (and shocking!) when
arranged so that they appear to be crawling across your table; try setting
up an overturned paper bag with the spiders scampering out.

What You Need

24 round chocolate cookies or licorice pinwheels

96 small, thin pretzel sticks

24 jelly beans

6 ounces (170 g) peanut butter (amount may vary)

Table knife

What You Do

Any round cookie, cracker, or candy will work for the body of the spider, though chocolate-colored foods are the most convincing; peruse the shelves of your supermarket for goodies with the most spidery texture.

• • • • •

Spread a generous portion of peanut butter on one side of a cookie and press another cookie on top to make a cookie sandwich. Break pretzels into 1-inch (2.5-cm) pieces, and stick pretzels between cookies into the peanut butter, four on each side, to make spider's legs. Cut jelly beans in half for the eyes, and use peanut butter to attach the jelly beans to the spiders. Makes about 12 spiders.

clever
costumes

Skeleton Costume

This simple costume is also a lesson in anatomy, with several important differences:
there's no test, and no one will check your accuracy!

What You Need

- Black sweatshirt/sweatpants
- Illustration of a human skeletal structure (encyclopedia, textbooks, and coloring books are good sources)
- Dressmaker's chalk, quilter's pencil, or any other marker that can be seen on dark fabric and easily erased
- Acrylic fabric paint, white and black
- Paint pen or small paintbrush
- Large paintbrush
- Newspaper or cardboard

designer: **TERRY TAYLOR**

What You Do

First, do some research and find a suitable illustration. Find one with a level of detail and difficulty to match your comfort (and skill) level. If you are prone to perfection, loosen up! For this project, whether every bone is in place and perfectly drawn is not important.

•••••••

Wash and dry the sweatshirt and sweatpants to remove any sizing in the fabric. Find a suitable flat work surface and lay out the shirt and pants. (A tabletop or the floor are excellent places to work.) Using dressmaker's chalk (or whatever marking tool you've selected), begin sketching out the skeleton design according to your illustration. At this point, lightly sketch a stick figure to indicate scale. The shoulder/arm area is a good place to begin. The chalk erases easily, so don't worry about mistakes.

•••••••

The hip girdle should begin almost at the top of the sweatpants; lightly sketch the outline of the hip girdle, then indicate with simple lines the length of the leg bones. You should allow an inch (2.5 cm) or so of blank space at the waist to allow the sweatshirt to hang over. Once you are satisfied with the proportions of your sketch, add details to the bones.

•••••••

Place folded newspaper or cardboard between the layers of the sweatsuit. Use a paint pen or a small brush to outline the sketched bones. Use a larger paintbrush to fill in bones. If you wish, shade the bones to give them a more three-dimensional effect. To do this, mix a small amount of black paint with white paint to make gray. Use the gray to shade, as desired.

•••••••

Remove the newspaper or cardboard, and allow the paint to dry thoroughly. Heat set fabric paints, if necessary, according to the paint manufacturer's instructions.

Dragon Costume

This fierce (and adorable) dragon is sure to be a roaring success among children and adults alike—and it requires absolutely no sewing.

designer: **KELLY DAVIS**

What You Need

- 2½ yards (2.3 m) of 60-inch-wide (152-cm) forest green felt
- 1 yard (.9 m) yellow felt
- Scrap of black felt
- Baseball cap
- Piece of cardboard, approximately 2 by 2 feet (.6 x .6 m)
- Plastic wiggle eyes (from craft store)
- Plastic jar lids or other plastic circles
- 2 feet (.6 m) ribbon
- Batting or other stuffing
- Hot-glue gun
- Green clothing (shirt, pants, and socks)
- Pencil

What You Do

Place baseball hat on a work surface, position green felt over hat, and cut out piece of felt to cover hat, adding 2 inches (5 cm) to the sides and 12 inches (30.5 cm) to the back. The extra fabric on the sides will be tucked under and glued; the extra fabric in back will be left hanging. Hot-glue felt onto hat.

Position one side of cardboard against the brim of the hat. Mark the cardboard with a semicircle to be fitted on top of brim against the front of hat. Cut out semi-circle where marked. Use the photograph to draw a snout shape on cardboard. Cut out snout.

Place cardboard snout on top of piece of felt and cut around shape, allowing 2 inches (5 cm) extra to tuck under. Use hot-glue gun to attach cardboard to bill of hat. Next, hot-glue felt over cardboard and loosely stuff end of snout with batting. Cut out two 3-inch (7.5-cm) green felt triangles. Fold and gather bottom of triangles to make ear shapes, and hot-glue in place on dragon head.

You will need plastic lids or cut-out plastic circles that are about ½ inch (1.5 cm) larger than the wiggle eyes. Use the plastic circles as templates to cut out four pieces of black felt. Glue two pieces of black felt to each of the plastic circles, then glue wiggle eyes on top of black felt.

To finish eyes, glue pieces (wiggle eyes, felt, and plastic circles) to front of hat, using a generous amount of hot glue at the base. Cut out teeth from yellow felt and hot-glue to underside of snout.

To make the dragon's body, first measure the person who will be wearing the costume. Measure from fingertip to fingertip across the back of the shoulders. Use the illustration provided to cut out the body section from green felt. Fold sides of tail section under to make the pointed end of the tail, and hot-glue edges of felt together. Stuff loosely with batting, then hot-glue the opening shut to keep batting in place.

Cut circles from yellow felt in different sizes, and hot-glue in a random pattern onto tail. Cut two arrow-shaped pieces from green felt. Sandwich tail between two pieces and hot-glue them together.

Cut two holes on each side of neck, and string ribbon through holes. Ribbon will serve to keep body of dragon in place. The person should wear green pants and shirt and wear green socks over regular shoes for dragon feet.

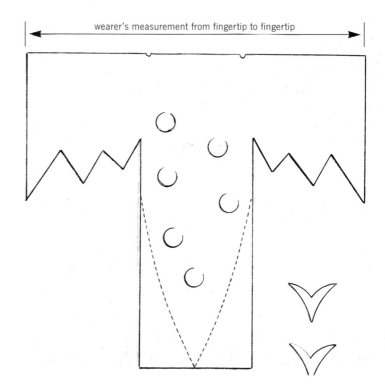

wearer's measurement from fingertip to fingertip

Trick-or-Treating Safety

HALLOWEEN is an exciting time for both kids and adults, and it is easy to let your guard down amidst all the merrymaking. Here are some tips to help you enjoy a safe Halloween.

ABOVE: Tiffany Marshall and Tamara Miller, also bedecked in pirate costumes, accompany their sons on early-evening trick-or-treating. See page 112 for costume intructions.

- Accompany young trick-or-treaters and send older children in groups with flashlights. Only venture out in your own neighborhood, or areas with which you are very familiar.

- Remind your kids never to enter a stranger's house; only take them to houses you know—and only if the porch lights are on.

- Don your children with reflectors before they go trick-or-treating. Use reflective tape creatively, on costumes and trick-or-treat bags, for example, to make sure your little demons are easily seen. Try to include glow-in-the-dark paint on handmade costumes.

- Masks can be dangerous when they cover mouths and eyes, so make sure they fit properly. Consider using face paint instead (see page 132).

- If you purchase a commercially made costume, choose one that is marked flame-retardant.

- Make sure costumes are short enough to prevent tripping. Do not allow children to wear costumes that obstruct vision, and always insist on comfortable, safe shoes.

- Use cardboard or other softer, safer materials to construct wands and other costume props, rather than metal or wood.

- Instruct your kids not to eat any of their treats until they get home and you have had a chance to inspect the food. Discard anything that looks odd (torn wrapping, for example) or has no wrapper at all.

- If you are stocked and ready for trick-or-treaters, be sure to turn your porch light and any exterior lights on. If you are going out or if you don't want trick-or-treaters, turn several interior lights on, but leave off exterior lights.

- Report any suspicious behavior or activity to the local police immediately.

ABOVE: Pam and Neal Beattie (Candler, NC) greet trick-or-treaters by constructing a spooky scene around the entryway of their home.

BELOW: A festive porch display, such as this one created by Tim Daly, is a great way to welcome trick-or-treaters.

- Exercise extreme caution when driving around on Halloween evening. Trick-or-treaters are not likely to be as aware of traffic as they should be, and many may be wearing dark costumes or masks that obstruct their vision.

- If you live in an area prone to high revelry and mischief from older kids, consider taking younger children trick-or-treating in the early evening before it becomes completely dark.

- One option is to take your children door-to-door as a group before dark, then go to a kid-safe Halloween party, such as those held at shopping malls, churches, and other organizations.

october trivia

Though October is the tenth month of the year, the word itself actually comes from the Latin *octobris mensis*, meaning "eighth month." It was so named because the original Roman year began in March.

Party Masks

A plastic mask base is a limitless canvas for a variety of lively feathers, leaves, and artificial flowers.

designer: **PAMELLA WILSON**

What You Need

- Plastic half masks
- Respirator mask (for beak mask)
- Feathers, silk flowers, and artificial leaves
- Strips of silk (for lining feather mask)
- Glitter paint (for feather mask)
- Hot-glue gun
- Elastic cord (for headpiece)
- Craft knife

What You Do

To make the feather mask, cut a beak from a respirator mask (available at hardware supply stores). Hot-glue the edges of the beak to the plastic mask base, and allow to dry thoroughly before feathers are applied. Begin to add feathers from the outside edge of the mask, securing each feather with small dots of hot glue. Continue to secure feathers until entire mask and beak are covered. Line the eye openings with cut strips of fabric; here the designer used strips of silk from an old tie. Glue the lining material on the inside of the mask's eye opening, then fold fabric through to outside of opening. Place dots of glitter paint randomly on silk fabric.

....

The leaf mask is made in essentially the same way as the feather mask, without the beak. Hot-glue artificial leaves to the mask from the outside edges in. To make the eyeholes, cut one leaf in half lengthwise with a craft knife, then make small cuts or notches in each leaf piece. Fold cut edges through eye openings, and hot-glue pieces in place on the inside of the mask.

....

To make the silk flower mask and headpiece, you will need three large artificial flowers and some silk leaves. Take two of the flowers and carefully pull apart layers of petals; you will use the outer four layers of the flowers for the main mask.

....

Begin by hot-gluing several leaves to the outer edges of the mask. Next, arrange each layer on the plastic half mask and hot-glue to the surface, securing with small dots of hot-glue on the underside of each flower. Cut out eye opening with a craft knife from the inside of the mask. Take a smaller flower layer and cut a third of the petals off to form eyelashes. Fold cut edge of flowers through the top of the eyehole and hot-glue in place.

....

The third flower (and foliage) will serve as the headpiece. First, bend the foliage into a pleasing fanlike shape, with the stem at the bottom. Tie and knot the ends of a length of elastic cord (available at fabric stores) to the stem. Hot-glue the last flower in the center of the silk foliage to complete the headpiece.

The She Vampire

IN THE YEARS FOLLOWING THE CIVIL WAR, a young girl named Sara lived on the banks of the Mississippi River. Now, Sara wasn't so young that she didn't have a hankerin' for love, and she had recently set her sights on Jacob, a handsome man from up the river. The only problem was that Jacob was hoping to marry a sweet, pretty maid from across the river, Emma Jean. Sara sat on the shady riverbank and cried every afternoon at four o'clock, when she saw the little riverboat dart from one landing to another. The riverboat's departure meant that Jacob was on his way to court Emma Jean.

One day, Sara's eyes were so red and puffy from her tears that she could hardly see, and she nearly fell into the river as she got up to leave. At that moment, she knew she must do something about her troubles. She had heard of a conjurin' woman who lived in an old house two miles up the river, and decided to pay her a visit. Maybe the conjurin' woman could call up some magic that would help her win Jacob.

That night after supper, when her chores were finished and her parents were in bed, Sara sneaked out of her window, walked the two miles to the run-down house, and knocked on the door. The huge, yellowed door creaked open a tiny crack, and a pair of green, catlike eyes peered out at her.

"What do you want from me?" A tall, thin woman in tattered white robes hissed at Sara through the crack. The woman was so thin and pale, she almost looked like a skeleton.

"Umm, well," Sara gulped. She tried to speak clearly, although her whole body trembled with fear. "I come from down the river, and I need some help winnin' a boy who's got eyes for another. I heard you was a conjurin' woman, and I just thought maybe you could give me a potion or something," she said to the eyes that stared at her out of the darkness. "I ain't got much money, but I can get you whatever you'd need, to be sure," Sara said.

At those words, the green cat eyes lit up with a bright glow. The woman smiled and opened the door wider. Sara wasn't sure that it was a nice smile, but it was a smile nonetheless. "You can get me whatever I need, you say?" the woman asked in her sinister voice.

Sara nodded her head, wondering if she would have to hunt down ingredients such as bat's eyes and toad's wart—things she'd always heard were used in magic potions.

"Won't you come in?" the conjurin' woman asked, offering another sly smile. As she stepped inside the door, Sara noticed two sharp, pointy teeth at either edge of the woman's smile, which gleamed a bright white in the dark hallway.

Sara awoke on the side of the road, halfway between her house and the conjurin' woman's house, just as the sun was beginning to rise. The sky was a faint gray as she opened her eyes and looked around. It took her a moment to realize where she was, and another few minutes to figure out how she'd gotten there. But soon the sky was a faint orange, and she knew she'd better get home and start her chores before her parents had a chance to figure out she wasn't there! She pushed herself off the ground and tried to get to her feet, but found she was so weak that she could hardly stand.

What was wrong with her? Was she sick? She wondered about her condition, growing ever more alarmed that her parents would soon realize she was missing. It took all the strength she had to walk the exhausting mile home, and she headed straight to the henhouse to collect the eggs for breakfast. At the breakfast table, seated across from her mother and father, Sara nearly nodded off to sleep on top of her pancakes, and hardly had the energy to lift her fork, though her body felt famished.

"Child, what in the world's the matter with you this morning?" her father asked. Her mother, too, looked concerned.

"Didn't you get any sleep last night, Sara?" she asked.

Sara nodded her head wearily, knowing she must not let them find out where she'd been. "Yes, I'm just a little sleepy, that's all," she said, laying her head on the table.

At that moment, her mother let out a shriek that sent her father's fist pounding down on the table in alarm, and Sara sat upright in her chair, now wide awake.

"Oh, my baby! My baby!" Her mother was crying loudly as she leapt from her chair and rushed over to Sara's seat. She pulled Sara's braid away from her neck to reveal to her husband what she had just seen: there, on the side of Sara's neck, were two long teeth marks on each side. Her father stared at the marks in horror, dropping his fork and knife and spilling coffee on the table as he jumped out of his chair.

"Who, who done this to you, girl?" he asked quietly, staring with wide eyes at his daughter's neck.

Sara had no idea what had happened to make her parents so frightened, and she simply stared back at them in confusion. "Done what?" she asked, looking from her mother to her father.

Her parents led her to the bathroom mirror and showed her the marks on her neck. As soon as Sara saw the marks, she screamed and collapsed in her mother's arms. When she awoke hours later, this time in her own bed, her parents were sitting nearby. Gathering her strength, she sat up in bed and began to tell them the truth about what had happened.

As soon as he heard the words "conjurin' woman," her father knew that an old legend he had heard as a child was true. His grandfather had told him and his brothers and sisters stories about an old woman who lived in the area. The woman, it was rumored, was a she-vampire; she lived off of other people's blood, his grandfather had said, and if she didn't get fresh, young blood every year, she would die. Sara's father had thought that this tale was nothing more than a scary story intended to make the children tremble around the fire on cold nights—but now he believed it.

Sara recovered and was on her feet again in a few days, but she abandoned her plan to use magic potions to get her man, and never walked the road to the conjurin' woman's house again. In fact, she found she didn't need to. As soon as he heard she was sick, Jacob came to visit Sara with a basket of flowers and a scarf to wear to hide the marks on her smooth, young neck. She wore the scarf on their wedding day the next spring, and kept it for years afterward, even after the marks had disappeared. So, it turned out that the conjurin' woman kept her side of the bargain; she helped Sara get her man after all.

Pirate Costumes

These costumes were created mainly from garments found in thrift stores, making this project an inexpensive undertaking. You probably have something appropriate in the back of your own closet.

What You Need

- Old clothes, such as wide-collared shirts, vests, pants, and caped jackets
- Boots (rubber rain boots work well)
- Accessories: scarves, plastic sword and hook, jewelry, eye patch, pirate's hat, and parrot
- Sewing machine or hot-glue gun
- 2-inch-wide (5-cm) self-stick, hook-and-loop tape (for attaching parrot)

killing vampires

According to legend, a vampire can only be killed by sunlight, a silver bullet, or by driving a stake through his heart while he sleeps. A couple of other options for ridding oneself of a vampire (though these will not kill him) are to hold a crucifix up to his face or to wear a necklace made of garlic.

What You Do

Adult pirate costumes can be made from inexpensive items from the thrift store: wide-collared shirts, over-sized black jackets, and blousy black pants. Scarves, jewelry, and plastic pirate hooks were used to accessorize the costumes. See page 106 for photograph of adult costumes.

· · · · · · · ·

The childrens' vests were made by cutting the sleeves out of jackets. The edges of these vests were hemmed on a sewing machine, but it is fine to leave the edges raw or fold under and secure edges with a hot-glue gun. Checkered pants work well for pirate's attire. Use the discarded sleeves from the jackets as the bottoms of the pirate pants; simply pull up over the calves of the pants and bunch fabric. Use a hot-glue gun to secure fabric in place, if necessary.

· · · · · · · ·

Any dark-colored boots will work for this costume. Accessorize the pirate costumes with plastic swords, lots of jewelry, scarves, and so forth. An eye patch can be purchased at any costume supply store, but can easily be handmade with a piece of black felt and elastic cording. Cut a circle of felt large enough to cover eye; either leave edges raw or hem with a sewing machine or a hot-glue gun. Staple the ends of elastic cording to each side of eye patch. Be creative!

· · · · · · · ·

The wooden parrots (available at floral supply stores or some craft stores) were attached with self-stick, hook-and-loop tape. Adhere hook-and-loop tape in place on vest and parrot, then connect tape pieces.

designer: **TAMARA MILLER**

Knitted Pumpkin Hat

This precious little hat is the perfect Halloween gift for your favorite toddler. This pattern is for a 6-month-old child; increase in multiples of eight stitches to adjust up or down in size.

designer: **MELANIE FRANCE**

What You Need

- Pumpkin-colored worsted-weight wool yarn, approximately 1 skein
- Brown worsted-weight wool yarn, approximately 1 skein
- Circular knitting needles, size 6
- Double-pointed needles, size 7

What You Do

Knitting abbreviations: **K:** KNIT; **INC:** INCREASE; **P:** PURL; **TOG:** TOGETHER

The gauge of this pattern is 5 stitches per inch (2.5 cm). Using the circular knitting needles (size 6), cast on 72 stitches with the pumpkin-colored yarn. Work the band by knitting in the round until work measures 1¼ inches (3 cm). When the band is complete, knit the next row: k2, inc 1 in the 3rd stitch, and repeat to the end of the round. This will give you 96 stitches.

Now, begin the body of the pumpkin hat, knit all rounds as follows: k6, p2, and repeat around hat until hat measures approximately 5 inches (12.5 cm).

For the crown of the pumpkin hat, decrease stitches as follows, changing to double-pointed needles when necessary:

ROW 1: K6, k2tog	**ROW 5:** K2, k2tog
ROW 2: K5, k2tog	**ROW 6:** K1, k2tog
ROW 3: K4, k2tog	**ROW 7:** K2 tog around
ROW 4: K3, k2tog	

To knit the stem, change to brown yarn and continue knitting in the round with the remaining stitches (12 stitches for 6-months size) until stem measures ¾ inch (2 cm)—or to suit your taste—and cut yarn, leaving a 4-inch (10-cm) tail. Thread yarn through stitches, taking each off the needle as you go. Work thread back through the first stitch you took off, and pull thread to inside and tie off. Tie off and trim yarn tail at the beginning of the hat band.

a jack of all pumpkins

The world's largest jack-o'-lantern was 827 pounds (375 kg) and was carved in Nut Tree, California, in 1992.

Bubble Bath Costume

Balloons are inexpensive and have endless possibilities with respect to costume design. This bubble bath costume is my favorite; another version is to use purple balloons, tapering the amount of balloons at the bottom of the costume (toward your feet) to create a convincing bunch of grapes.

What You Need

- 9-inch (23-cm) round, white balloons, about 35
- Small safety pins, one for each balloon
- White long-sleeved shirt
- White pants
- Accessories: bath cap, rubber ducky, and scrub brush
- Tape

What You Do

Blow up balloons. You will need enough to cover the front of shirt and arms, or about 35 balloons; the exact number depends on the size of the balloons. (Do not cover the back of the shirt with balloons, because you will be unable to sit down.)

• • • • •

Using small safety pins, attach the knotted ends of the balloons to the white shirt, making sure the entire surfaces of the shirt and sleeves are covered. Do not wear shirt while you are doing this; it is highly recommended that you take shirt to party, then put it on over what you are wearing, as it is easy to pop the balloons.

• • • • •

Tape a rubber ducky to a balloon in front, wear a shower cap (or wrap your hair in a towel), and carry a scrub brush for added effect.

designer: **SUSAN EDWARDS**

Last-Minute Costumes

HERE ARE SOME COSTUME IDEAS for the reveller who just can't get it together until the last minute—or who doesn't want to spend a lot of time (or a fortune) on a Halloween costume.

The Old Standards

CLOWN: Make a small cut in a ping-pong ball, paint it red, and voila! You have a convincing nose. (Ears can also be made in this way.) Wear white gloves and baggy, colorful clothes, and paint your face.

SKELETON: Freehand a skeleton on a black garbage bag with white paint. You can also create the design with white tape, wrapping the tape around your arms as well. Cover face with white face paint, and use black paint around eyes.

WITCH: A black witch hat can be easily had at almost any store that carries costumes. Paint your face white and use a black eyeliner pencil to make a large mole. Dress all in black and carry a broom.

MUMMY: Dress in white and wrap yourself entirely in toilet tissue or cheesecloth. Paint your face white, then puff white face powder on for an extra mummified look.

GHOST: Drape an old white sheet over your head and make holes for your eyes and nose. (Trim the sheet around the bottom, if necessary, to prevent tripping over it.) Wear a hat (over the sheet) to keep the sheet in place.

PAPER BAG MASK: You'll be surprised at how effective a simple paper bag can be when embellished with colored markers. Cut holes in the bag for your eyes and mouth. Hot-glue ears or any other embellishments to the bag. Spray-paint the bag silver for a scary alien mask.

ROBOT: Cut holes in cardboard box for arms and legs, and a hole in one end of a smaller cardboard box for the robot's head. Use light sticks or pipe cleaners for antennae. Either spray-paint cardboard silver or cover with aluminum foil.

Frighteningly Easy Costumes

HOODLUM: Wear tight black clothing and gloves, and pull a pair of panty hose over your head. Carry a toy gun.

ARTIST: Smudge different colors of paint on a white smock and beret. Create an artist's palette out of cardboard and colored markers and carry a large paintbrush.

PUMPKIN: Stuff a pumpkin-printed garbage bag with newspaper and wear with black tights.

FOREST: Pin or hot-glue leaves, twigs, branches, and other natural materials to green or brown clothing.

ZEBRA: Wear a black body suit (or any other tight-fitting black clothing), and use wide masking tape to create zebra stripes.

LITTLE RED RIDING HOOD: If you own a hooded red coat, you're in luck! Wear the coat (with the hood up, of course) and carry of basket of "goodies."

THE SUNDAY PAPER: Dress all in white or black and use safety pins to attach pieces of newspaper all over you.

SKIN DIVER: Wear a tight wet suit or track suit, goggles, and flippers. Slick hair back.

TOURIST: Wear the most colorful, wildly printed shirt you can find (thrift stores are great sources) and long shorts. Don sunglasses and a sun visor, and rub white sunscreen (or white face paint) across your nose. Hang a camera around your neck, and carry a guidebook.

continued on next page

Last-Minute Costumes, continued

SPORTS STAR: If you have any old sports jerseys and sports equipment around your house, such as hockey, football, or baseball gear, you can easily create a sports star costume. For a more convincing costume, cut lettering out of felt and hot-glue the star's name to the back of the costume.

FLOOR LAMP: OK, it may be a stretch, but a lamp shade resting on your head may be enough to get you into a costumes-only party. Pin an electric cord (with a plug on one end) to your backside.

FIRECRACKER: Wear a red top, attach a length of rope to your head, and wrap yourself in bubble wrap.

MONEY TREE: Wear all green clothing, and glue or pin fake money (from a board game) to clothing.

Crazy Concept Costumes

BOSTON TEA PARTY: Dress in all one color (white works well), and use safety pins to attach tea bags to your clothing. Carry a sign that says "No Taxation Without Representation."

BOUNCED CHECK: Connect two rectangular pieces of cardboard with two lengths of string; make two centered holes on one long side of each piece of cardboard, and tie ends of string through holes. Place cardboard over head, allowing one string to rest on each shoulder. Once the cardboard pieces fit well across your shoulders, use thick permanent markers to draw on the cardboard to create a check design; imitate a check exactly, with the endorsement on the back piece of cardboard. With a red marker, write "Insufficient Funds" across front of check. Carry a ball—and bounce it frequently to get the point across.

LIVE WIRE: Dress all in one color, and wrap yourself entirely in colored electric wires. Carry sparklers.

BASKET CASE: Dress all in brown, and pin baskets all over clothing.

SHOOTING STARS: Dress all in tight-fitting black clothes. Cut stars from yellow construction paper, and pin to clothing. Carry a toy gun.

great green slime

Set out a bowl of not-quite-set green gelatin. Don't cut it into neat squares, but slop it randomly into the container.

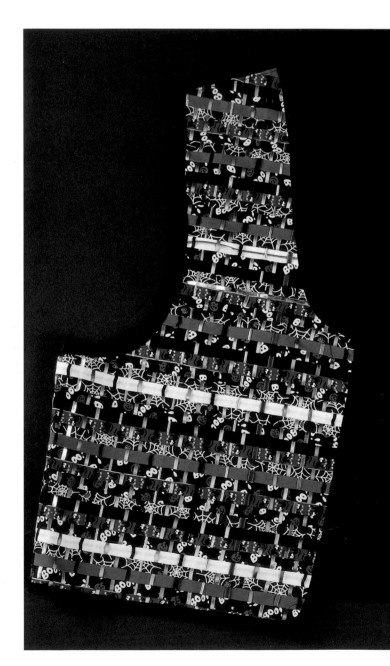

Halloween Ribbon Vest

Remnants of small-print Halloween fabric and colored bias tape are put to good use in this splendid ribbon vest.

designer: **BONNIE HALL**

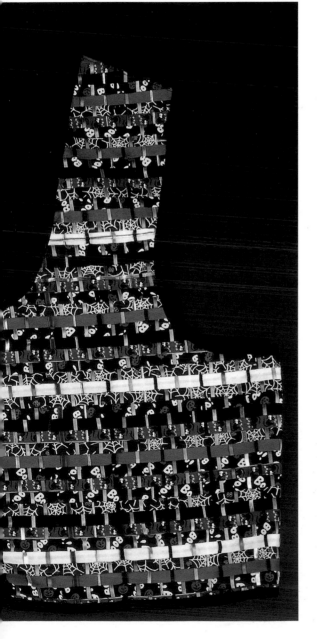

What You Need

- Vest pattern in your size
- Fusible backing
- Pin board
- Straight pins
- Approximately 32 yards (29 m) of ¼-inch (.5-cm) double-folded bias tape or double-folded small-print Halloween fabric (or a combination of both): quantity depends on size of pattern
- ⅛-inch (.3-cm) ribbon in three to five complementary colors, between 30 and 35 yards (27 and 32 m), depending on size of pattern
- ¼-inch (.5-cm) bias tape maker
- Steam iron
- Sewing machine

What You Do

You may use either a commercially made pin board (available in fabric stores) or make your own by drawing ½-inch (1.5-cm) grid lines on a piece of corrugated cardboard.

• • • • •

Begin by cutting fabric into ½-inch (1.5-cm) strips. (These strips do not need to be cut on the bias.) Work strips through bias tape maker, and press the folded strips with a steam iron as they emerge from tape maker. (A bias tape maker is a gadget that folds the bias strips as you press. It is quite inexpensive.)

• • • • •

Cut fusible backing slightly larger than vest pattern. Position vest pattern on pin board, lining up sides of vest against parallel lines. (The vest pattern will help align the fusible foundation.) Position fusible backing over vest pattern, with adhesive side up.

• • • • •

The smaller ribbons will be woven vertically, and the larger fabric pieces will be woven horizontally. First, use the grid to position the ribbons to the vertical grid, placing a pin at the end of each row as you work. Next, weave the fabric ribbons and/or bias tape over and under the ribbons, alternating fabric colors between each row. Again, pin each piece.

• • • • •

Once the weaving is complete, move the entire (pinned) project (including the pin board) to the ironing board, and press according to the fusible backing manufacturer's instructions. When the entire piece is finished, remove the pins, trim the edges, and stitch around the entire outside edge of the vest with a basting stitch.

• • • • •

Repeat the procedure for the opposite vest piece, remembering to flip the pattern over and using the completed side as a guide for the order of the strips. Complete the vest according to the pattern instructions.

Living in the Land of the Dead

LONG LONG AGO, the Chinook tribe settled on a flat plain between the great water and the great mountains. Soon after they had built their lodges on the plain, the old chief of the largest village passed away, and his young son, Lone Feather, rose up to take his place.

Lone Feather was brave and strong and just, and he felt proud to be the chief of the village. However, he also felt very lonely. One afternoon, while visiting the chief of a neighboring village, a striking young woman caught Lone Feather's eye. Her name was Blue Jay, because a blue jay had been singing outside her father's window the morning she was born. Lone Feather fell

in love with Blue Jay instantly, and she with him, and after four full moons, they began to plan for their marriage ceremony. They would be married in the spring, when the streams rushed with water from the snow melting in the mountains.

As the streams began to rush with the clear, cold water from the melting snow, however, Lone Feather's head began to get hot with fever, and his body weak with sickness. He could not leave his lodge for many days, and Blue Jay sat by his side, singing songs to pray for his recovery. On the first full moon after Lone Feather fell ill, his eyes closed a final time, and his spirit left his body to follow the spirits of his ancestors to the Land of the Dead.

Blue Jay and the people of all the villages mourned the death of the young chief, and they took many canoes to carry his body to one of the remote burial islands. The people erected a high platform of poles and placed Lone Feather's body upon it, then hurried back to the canoes and paddled home. They did not dare to linger on a burial island.

When the streams were rushing with high waters and spring had finally arrived, Blue Jay could not bring herself to smile or sing with the rest of her tribe. She still mourned for Lone Feather and was very sad. On the next full moon, Lone Feather came to her in a dream and told her that he, too, missed her, and was very sad. He could not find peace among his ancestors in the Land of the Dead without her.

At daybreak, Blue Jay hurried to tell her father about her dream. Her father listened, and agreed that she should go to Lone Feather. That night, after the rest of the village was asleep, Blue Jay and her father paddled a canoe far up the river into the burial islands to the most sacred island of all, the secret place of the Dead, where none of the Living dared to go. In their canoe, Blue Jay and her father could only find their way through the darkness and thick fog by following the distant sounds of drumming and singing coming from the celebrating of the Dead. They were dancing and sounded joyous.

Blue Jay's father dropped her off on the shore of the island, and she followed the music to the circle of the Dead. Her ancestors greeted her with hugs and shouts of joy, until they realized she was still a member of the Living.

"What are you doing here?" they demanded. "None of the Living are allowed on the island of the Dead," they told her. Just as a tear began to slide down her cheek, Lone Feather recognized her from his place in the crowd of the dancing Dead and ran to her. With a shout of joy, they fell into each other's arms. Lone Feather convinced the tribal ancestors to allow Blue Jay to remain among the Dead, and they agreed. The rest of the night was spent rejoicing and dancing to celebrate her arrival.

Just before dawn, Lone Feather led Blue Jay quickly away from the circle of fire and dancers toward his lodge, where they laid down on mats to sleep. But, as the sun rose, she could hear blue jays singing outside the window, and she left her mat to greet the dawn, as she did every day at home.

Blue Jay stepped outside of the lodge to sing with the birds, but as soon as she did she stopped and stared around her in horror. She saw skeletons lying and sitting in the grass before her, and in the distance she could see piles of bones strewn around the dance circle. She turned and looked back at Lone Feather on the sleeping mat, and he too was a skeleton! Daylight had reduced the Dead to bones, skeletons waiting to reawaken at dusk. Surrounded by stillness and skeletons, Blue Jay sat alone all day, frightened by her new world.

As the sun set behind the clouds, the Dead rose from the ground and began to sing and dance again, just as they had been doing the night before. Lone Feather was hers again, in the flesh, and she was happy. After many full moons had passed, Blue Jay and Lone Feather had a son, and their lodge was filled with blessings. But Blue Jay needed one thing to be truly happy: she wanted to take her son back to the Land of the Living to show him to her mother and father.

Everyone among the Dead thought this was a bad idea, and told her she must not return. Yet, Blue Jay was stubborn. She would go. As she left, one of the wise elders gave her some words of advice: "Do not let anyone in the Land of the Living gaze upon your child for ten days," she said. Blue Jay nodded her head, wrapped her baby in a blanket, and paddled a canoe back down the river toward her village.

When she arrived, her people would not speak to her. They thought she was an evil spirit returning from the Land of the Dead and did not trust her. However, her parents welcomed her home and took her into their lodge to celebrate her homecoming. When Blue Jay explained that they could not look upon her son for ten days, her mother was suspicious. That afternoon, while Blue Jay slept during the strongest hours of daylight, (which now hurt her eyes, having grown accustomed to seeing only at night), her mother sneaked into her room to peek at the baby. She picked him up off his place beside his mother on the floor, and folded back a corner of the blanket.

Inside, she saw a tiny white skeleton, and immediately dropped the bundle onto the floor out of fright! Blue Jay awoke at the sound of her baby's bones crashing to the floor, and she cried large tears as she gathered them, one by one, back into the blanket. For four days and nights her son remained nothing but bones, and, in a state of despair, Blue Jay left her village and paddled back to the island of the Dead.

She arrived just as the sun was setting, and as she pulled her canoe on shore, she heard a soft cry come from the bundle in the blanket. She pulled back a corner of the blanket, and saw that her son had become a baby again. Lone Feather hurried to her canoe, and they smiled and sang to their son as they walked toward the fire and the circle of dancers. That night, the tribal elders on the island of the Dead made a decision and declared that never again would anyone be allowed to pass from the Land of the Living to the Land of the Dead.

Jester's Hat

A dramatic jester hat makes a striking costume almost on its own—the only other things you need are baggy, fun clothes and some colorful beads.

What You Need

- 4 pieces of colored felt, approximately 1½ x 1 feet (.5 x .3 m)
- Pattern (see below)
- Piece of 1-inch (2.5-cm) elastic, approximately 7 inches or 18 cm (see below)
- ¼-inch (.5-cm) ribbon, approximately 10 inches (25.5 cm)
- ½-inch (1.5-cm) bells

What You Do

Using the pattern provided, cut out the four pieces of different-colored felt, adding a 1-inch (2.5-cm) seam allowance. Next, begin to sew the pieces together, using thread that matches one of the four colors of felt. Sew from the outer corner of each piece and work toward the tops (peaks). The top piece of each section should come together exactly to form the top of the hat. When you sew the corners at the ends, insert a 2-inch (5-cm) piece of ribbon that has been threaded with a bell, and sew into seam. Do not finish off bottom seam yet.

• • • • • • •

Place hat on head of person who will be wearing it to determine how much elastic is needed. For most adult head sizes, one strip of elastic sewn into the bottom of one colored felt section is enough. For smaller heads, use more elastic. You can line the entire base of the hat with elastic, if necessary. Sew the elastic into the seam.

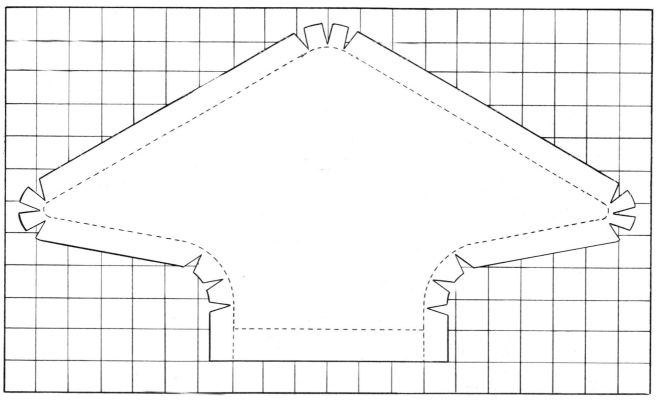

ENLARGE PATTERN 147%

designer: **HEATHER SMITH**

Fish Tank Costume

A playful fish-filled aquarium can be put together in just a few hours, making this a quick and easy costume—not to mention an unusual one.

What You Need

- Cardboard or lattice board
- Printed fish fabric, approximately 3 yards (2.7 m), or blue fabric, fabric paints, and fish stencils
- Black spray paint
- Tape measure
- Staple gun
- Black electrical tape
- Craft glue
- Blue clothing: shirt and tights
- Optional accessories: hair gel, fish net, aquarium plants or seaweed, snorkel gear, or plastic fish

What You Do

The frame for this tank was made from cardboard that was cut to the wearer's dimensions. Alternatively, you could use strips of lattice board for a more sturdy frame. Also note that the preprinted fabric was used, but you can easily paint fish (either freehand or with stencils) on plain blue fabric.

....

Measure the person who will wear the costume across the shoulders, then from one shoulder to about mid-calf. The weight of the frame will rest on the shoulders, so measure exactly. Also determine a comfortable width, from front to back, for the frame. Keep in mind that a great-looking costume should also be comfortable, and that the costume should not impede mobility.

....

Cut the cardboard into 3-inch (7.5-cm) strips. Cut four of the strips to the shoulder-to-calf measurement, four to the shoulder-to-shoulder measurement, and six to the front-to-back width. Spray-paint each piece black and let dry thoroughly.

....

Once the cardboard has dried, assemble the pieces to form the front and back panels. Measure and cut fabric to fit inside the panel, adding an extra inch (2.5 cm). Staple fabric to front and back panels. Attach a shorter board at the top and bottom between these panels to form each side. You may need to use craft glue and black electrical tape to secure these pieces. (There will be two short boards left over.) Cut fabric as you did for the front and back pieces, and staple in place. Cut out a hole at the top for each arm. Use strips of black electrical tape to conceal staples.

....

For extra support, use the remaining two pieces of cardboard, which are cut to fit from front to back across the top of the shoulder. Attach them to the top piece on the front and back with tape or staples. These extra boards will hold the tank on the person and should rest securely on the shoulders. Try on the costume and check for fit; make any needed adjustments.

....

Wear blue clothing under the fish tank and carry the accessories of your choice. Use hair gel to slick back hair so that it appears the wearer has just emerged from the water.

Making a Mummy

TO MAKE a mummy, stuff clothes with newspaper and wrap stuffed shape with gauze. A polystyrene head form (available at wig shops) works wonderfully as the head shape; make sure you include shoes as well. Fold arms in front (on the chest) of the mummy before wrapping.

Bag Costumes

Large feed bags from a local nursery make great (and inexpensive) bases for a variety of "bag" costumes. Here, we've chosen a colorful popcorn bag and a grocery bag. The grocery bag also has the advantage of being ecologically friendly, since it is made almost entirely out of recycled materials from around your house.

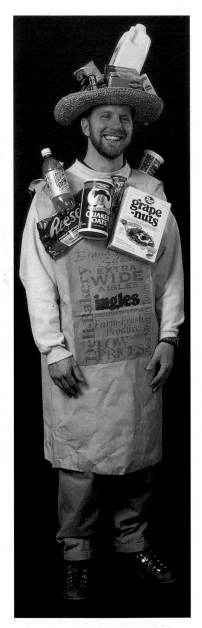

What You Need

- Large, heavy-duty bag
- Hot-glue gun

for popcorn bag:

- White spray paint
- Red acrylic paint (for stripes)
- Blue acrylic paint (for lettering)
- Baseball cap
- Aluminum foil
- Popcorn (amount will vary)
- Red shirt

for grocery bag:

- Brown spray paint
- Bag from local grocery store
- Wide-brimmed straw sun hat
- Neutral-colored shirt

designers: **ANDREA JERNIGAN AND BUTCH BASSETT**

What You Do

These designers got empty seed bags from a local nursery, but other types of heavy-duty bags will work just as well. For small children, regular brown paper grocery bags will be sufficient, though less durable. (Another option is to sew a simple bag out of burlap or any other sturdy fabric; if you choose to do this, you will need to stuff the bag with newspaper.) Cut holes for arms and head in the paper bag, then cut a neat edge on bottom of the bag.

• • • • •

To make the popcorn bag, spray-paint the entire bag white, and allow to dry thoroughly. Paint wide horizontal stripes with red acrylic paint. When the stripes are dry, sketch the lettering on the bag, then paint sketched letters with blue acrylic paint. Cover a baseball hat with aluminum foil, scrunching the foil around the hat to create a pleasing shape. Hot-glue popcorn over the entire surface of the hat and to the top of the popcorn bag. Wear a red shirt with this costume.

• • • • •

To make the grocery bag, spray-paint the entire surface of the paper bag brown. (The bag may be brown already, in which case painting is unnecessary.) Cut the front of a local grocery store bag—the side that has the store logo—and hot-glue to the front of the bag. (You can also glue one to the back, if you wish.) Hot-glue empty boxes and other food containers to the top of the bag (where the shoulders will be). Glue smaller containers to a wide-brimmed straw sun hat. Wear a neutral-colored shirt with this costume.

Picnic Table Costume

Impress your fellow party-goers or trick-or-treaters by transforming a square cardboard box into a delightful picnic table costume. This easy table design can be adapted to create a number of other table-themed costumes, such as a card table, a conference table, or a kitchen table.

What You Need

- Square cardboard box, approximately 3 x 3 feet (.9 x .9 m)
- Square vinyl tablecloth (red and white checkerboard print is ideal)
- Permanent black marker
- Picnic foods/supplies (paper plate, plate basket, hot dog, chips, ketchup and mustard bottles, salt and pepper shakers, and so forth)
- Red shirt
- Hot-glue gun (or duct tape)
- Scissors
- Picnic basket (optional)

What You Do

Trim off the top half of the cardboard box, leaving a 3-inch (7.5-cm) edge; the edge makes the cardboard look like a table-top. (The edge should be long enough to rest on the wearer's shoulders, while also allowing arms to be free for movement.)

· · · · · · ·

Cut the tablecloth to hang down several inches (5 cm) lower than the edge of the box. Cut circle in top of box for head. (Arms will remain free under box.) Hot-glue or tape table-cloth to top of box, cutting head hole in center of tablecloth to match hole in cardboard.

· · · · · · ·

Affix picnic supplies (see materials list) to top of table with hot glue or tape. Use a permanent black marker to draw a line of ants marching up the side of the tablecloth to the plate. Wear a red shirt underneath picnic table. Carry a picnic basket, if you wish; it will come in handy, whether you are collecting or handing out treats.

designer: **MERCEDES RIOS-YOUNG**

how far can you chunk a punkin'?

Every year in Delaware, the World Championship Punkin' Chunkin' contest is held. The record-holder in the under-ten youth division tossed an 8- to 10-pound (3.6 to 4.5 kg) pumpkin 128 feet, 2 inches (39 m, 5 cm) in 1993. All proceeds from the Punkin' Chunkin' go to charity.

Bumblebee Costume

A brightly colored shirt and a black hat made of synthetic fleece will keep your busy bumblebee warm on Halloween night. This costume requires only basic sewing skills.

What You Need

for the body piece:

- Black synthetic fleece (amount depends on size of wearer)
- Yellow synthetic fleece or reflective tape
- Black turtleneck (optional) and black pants or tights
- Gold pipe cleaners (for wings), approximately 20

for the hat:

- Black synthetic fleece, approximately 1 x 2 feet (.3 x .6 m)
- Length of black string
- 2 large black, yellow, or gold pom-pons (or polystyrene balls)
- 2 black, yellow, or gold pipe cleaners

What You Do

To make the body piece, first take the measurements of a shirt that fits the child loosely; you will use these measurements to cut two pieces of black synthetic fleece for the front and back pieces. Allow an extra inch (2.5 cm) of fabric for the seam.

·······

Cut the yellow synthetic fleece into 2-inch-wide (5-cm) strips that are long enough to fit horizontally across the body. Alternatively, you could use reflective tape for the stripes, which will increase your child's visibility at night. To create the bee stripes, sew the stripes to the black synthetic fleece, leaving 1½ inches (4 cm) between each stripe. Make sure the stripes meet each other, back and front, at the seams.

Place the two pieces of fabric, with right (striped) sides together and sew the pieces together along each edge. If you would like to make a vest (and wear a black turtleneck underneath), simply hem the arm and neck holes with a 1-inch (2.5-cm) seam. To make the arms, measure the length and diameter (at both the top and the bottom) of the wearer's arm, add several inches (5 cm) to each measurement, and cut two pieces of synthetic fleece for the arms. Sew the long sides of the pieces with right sides together (to form a tube), and trim the excess fabric. Stitch the side of the arm pieces with the largest diameter to the body piece and hem the sleeves.

designer: **LISA COLBY**

You can either hem the neck hole or make another tube for a turtleneck. To make the tube, measure the neck hole of the body piece and cut a 4-inch (10-cm) piece of black synthetic fleece to that measurement. Sew together to form a tube as with the arms, and stitch tube to neck. (You should frequently try the costume on the wearer during this process to assure a good fit.) Turn right side out.

• • • • • • •

Bend and connect gold pipe cleaners to form two connected wings and stitch the wings to the costume. The child should wear black pants or tights under the body piece.

To make the hat, measure the child's head and cut the black synthetic fleece to the appropriate width, adding an extra 1 inch (2.5 cm) for the seam. Sew the synthetic fleece lengthwise, with wrong sides together, to make a tube. Gather the top of the tube and secure with a string. Cut the gathered material to create fringe.

• • • • • • •

To make the antennae, wrap one end of each pipe cleaner around a pom-pon. (Polystyrene balls painted yellow or black also work well for the tops of the antennae.) Sew the other end of each pipe cleaner to the hat, on opposite sides, so the pom-pons are higher than the fringe.

Face-Painting Basics

FACE PAINT can transform a mediocre costume into a fabulous one. In fact, a well-painted face can even stand alone and serve as a last-minute costume. It's really easy if you have some water-based paint and a few inexpensive tools.

SUPPLIES

Water-based paint is the best choice for face painting, primarily because it is easily washed off with warm water and soap. In addition, it is easier on sensitive skin. If you are buying paint for only one costume, you will probably want to buy only a few individual colors. Individual colors come in separate pots (which require added water) or in cream-based form in squirt bottles. (Creamy paint is more greasy.) If you have several faces to paint or want to experiment with color, invest in a full color palette. Cream-based paint colors can be lightened, darkened, or blended to create new colors. Always read manufacturer's instructions thoroughly before using any paint product.

Invest in at least two brushes: a large one to fill in large areas and a small one for detail work. A medium brush is also useful (though not essential) for everything in between. Paintbrushes work, but professional makeup brushes are even better, though more expensive. Make sure the bristles are not too hard. You will also need makeup sponges to apply makeup, especially the base color. (Bath sponges cut into pieces will work.) An eyebrow pencil is an excellent tool for small marks, and a stipple sponge creates the perfect five-o'clock shadow.

THE BASICS

Wash face, rinse, and dry thoroughly. Rinse by splashing cold water on the face; it closes pores and helps prevent makeup from absorbing into the skin. It helps to apply a moisturizer before you begin painting, as it will create a smoother surface and make the paint easier to remove.

Sketch the design onto a piece of paper for reference. In general, the more simple the design, the more pronounced the effect. That being said, any design you choose should be exaggerated. Arch eyebrows high and layer colors for a more striking impression. Once you have decided on a design and chosen the color palette, apply the base coat of paint (see right). If you are not using creamy paint, wet the sponge and squeeze out excess water. Press the sponge to the paint pot, then dab the sponge over the entire surface of the face, beginning in the middle of the face. Last, sponge the eye area; make sure the eyes are closed. If you are using cream-based paint, squirt some paint onto a clean surface and apply paint with the sponge—no water required.

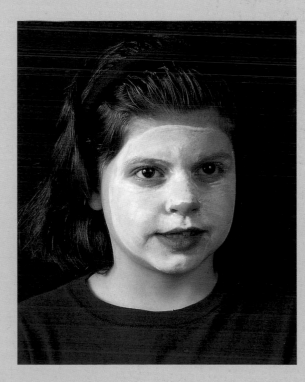

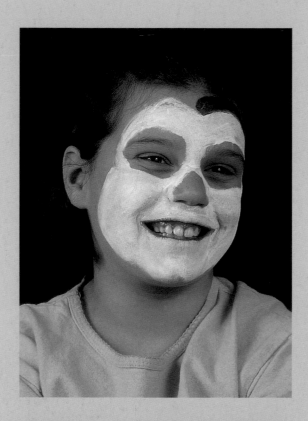

Use the paintbrushes to paint the design. Dip the brush in water, then the first color of paint, and begin to draw the design. It will take some experimenting to determine how much paint to leave on the brush. Be conservative in the amount of makeup you apply; it is always easier to apply more than to remove. Keep the brush moving while you paint to prevent a wobbly line. Take your time, be patient, and keep at it. With most face-painting designs, the eyes are the focal point. Some paint colors are more irritant to eye areas than others, so read the manufacturer's instructions carefully.

One effective strategy is to paint the entire face white and create black circles around the eyes (see photographs at left). This is a great beginning for a variety of scary faces: ghost, witch, monster, and ghoul. Then individualize with other colors of paint and a small paintbrush. Use flesh-colored paint as a base for

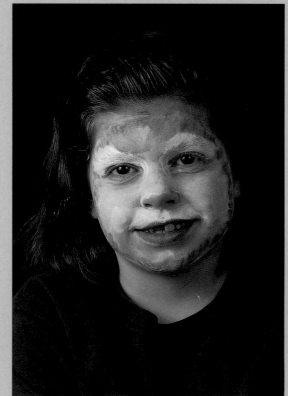

more realistic costumes, such as a princess, doll, bride, or celebrity. Then draw on the other features—exaggerated, of course—with a small paintbrush.

Once you've had some practice, experiment with blending paint. After the base coat has dried, use a dry makeup sponge to dab on the second color (see photograph [right] on page 134). (Your fingers will also work.) Gently blend with the sponge. Be careful not to wipe off the base coat. Apply darker colors first, then create effects with lighter paint.

Once the design is complete, powder the entire face with cosmetic or baby powder to set the paint. Do not rub the powder in, though, as it will mess up the design.

HAIR COLOR

First, style the hair as desired. Dip a sponge into water, then paint. Dab it over the surface of the hair. Use paintbrushes to color in details (gray hair, patterns, and streaks). A toothbrush is a superb tool for brushing out paint blobs. Face paint can also be applied to wigs.

FACE-PAINTING ACCESSORIES

False facial hair is a striking companion to face paint. Create beards, moustaches, and even a disgusting sprig of hair emerging from a witch's mole. It is available at costume shops and is easily applied (and removed) to the face with spirit gum—a glue for false hair—or eyelash adhesive.

Try sprinkling glitter on the painted face—it will stick—or use glitter paint or gel. Mold wax or putty into noses, warts, scars, or other special effects, and apply with spirit gum. These can be removed with alcohol or acetone. Wigs, glasses, jewelry, scarves, and hats are also excellent props.

CAUTIONS

- Never paint over open sores, abrasions, or rashes.

- Be very careful with paint around eyes. Eyes should be closed and relaxed while face painting. Take care not to get paint in the eyes. Should paint get in your eyes, flush with cold water. When you paint around the eyes, take care that the person is looking away from the paintbrush.

- Always test for allergic reactions before you begin. Apply a small amount of paint to the forearm the night before, and watch for symptoms of irritation. If you experience irritation, do not use. If sensitivity occurs anytime while using face paint, discontinue use immediately.

- Since face paint contains color pigments, it may stain clothing.

- To clean up, first wipe off the paint with a cosmetic sponge, tissue, or cotton ball, then wash face thoroughly with soap and water, and apply moisturizer.

frightening fun

Creepy Halloween Cards

Finding hair-raising images to photocopy is fun when creating these enchanting handmade cards. Depending on the chosen images, the cards can convey a playful Halloween spirit or an understated, eerie message.

What You Need

- Blank cards or sturdy paper
- Photocopied Halloween images
- Selection of decorative and handmade paper in black, orange, and gold
- White craft glue or hot-glue gun
- Ribbon

What You Do

Cover blank cards or sturdy paper with decorative paper, and secure paper with glue. Use several types and colors of paper for each card: one for the front cover, another for the inside, and so forth. Make sure to cover both the inside and outside surfaces. Copy selected images from anatomy books (skulls and skeletons), horror tales (monsters, castles, and gargoyles), or any other source, and glue the images onto the front of the folded card form.

. . . .

Embellish as you wish with ribbon and paper scraps. One of the best aspects of this project is the potential use of scraps and odds and ends. Dig into those boxes of decorative paper, ribbons, and other trinkets.

. . . .

NOTE: The postal service charges extra for mail that exceeds the general postal requirements for first class mail. Because of the extra materials used in these cards, they tend to weigh more.

designer: **NICOLE TUGGLE**

"Halloweeno" and "Hallo-Words" Games

These simple games are amusing Halloween party activities—and a great learning opportunity—since children practice letters and learn new words in the process. Reward the winners with candy or colored pencils for a game that is truly in the Halloween spirit.

designer: **BARBARA STEPP**

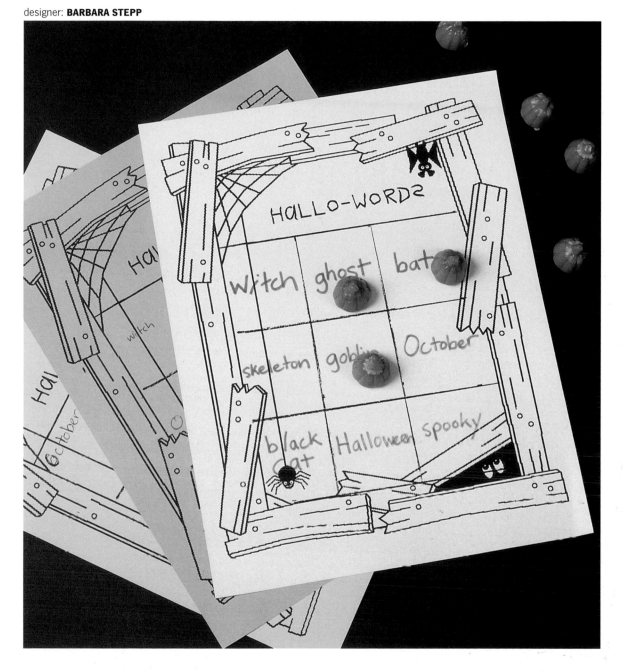

What You Need

- Squares of card stock or construction paper in Halloween colors
- Permanent black marker or computer-generated border
- Candy for game markers (candy corn or candy pumpkins)
- Erasable colored pencils

What You Do

For both games, create game boards with colored card stock or construction paper. Decorate the borders of one white sheet with a black marker. (You may also use a computer-generated border, as the designer has done here.) Each game will need a grid with nine squares. Once you are happy with the design and the grid, photocopy it onto additional sheets of paper.

· · · · · · · ·

Now that you have the basic game boards, you will need to decide which game you want to play. For Halloweeno, print the letters from the word "Halloween" inside the squares—one letter per square, as shown in the photograph. Each game board should have a different combination of letters. The center square is a free square and should always have the letter "O." To help young children learn their letters, ask each of them to print their own letters onto the grid. Create as many combinations as you have players, remembering to leave the "O" in the center square.

Determine the ground rules for your version of Halloweeno. The winner could be the first to fill all four corners, a vertical line, a horizontal line, and so forth. Designate someone to call out letters randomly (or pick them from a hat). When a letter is called, the player places a piece of candy on the correct square. (Letting the children know they can eat the candy after the game is over makes for a particularly enthusiastic crowd.)

· · · · · · · ·

Hallo-Words is played in essentially the same way, except Halloween-related words are used instead of letters. Either photocopy the blank grids and allow the children to fill in the words, or fill in the words ahead of time. Use erasable pencils so that game boards can be reused. Make one word be the free space in the center as before. Some great words to use are Halloween, witch, skeleton, black cat, bat, goblin, October, spooky, and ghost.

Other Halloween Game Ideas for Children

CHILLING CHECKERS: Create a game board by gluing squares of black and orange construction paper to a piece of sturdy construction paper. There are a variety of items you can use for game pieces: plastic spiders, miniature pumpkins, marshmallow ghosts, wax teeth, and so forth. For added effect, cover the game board with artificial spider webs!

PIN THE NOSE ON THE PUMPKIN: Cut a pumpkin out of orange poster paper. Cut a nose shape out of black poster paper, and attach double-sided masking tape to the back. Draw eyes and mouth on pumpkin with a black marker, if desired. Secure pumpkin shape to the wall. Blindfolded players try to attach nose in the appropriate spot. The player with the best effort gets a prize.

GHOST BOWLING: Cover 10 toilet tissue tubes with white tissue paper and draw ghost eyes on each with a black marker. Secure tissue to tube with several dabs of white craft glue. Have children use a softball to knock over as many tubes as they can at one time. This is a great game to help children practice counting!

PUMPKIN RING TOSS: A fun Halloween version of horseshoes is to arrange pumpkins at various distances from a starting point. The kids then try to throw a hula hoop around the pumpkins. Use a colored marker to indicate the number of points the player receives from each pumpkin (by writing the number on the pumpkin, with the pumpkins located farther away having the highest value).

The Hungry Snake Game

Decorating and coloring the game board is part of the fun in this terrific game.
All you need is paper, markers, and some energetic and imaginative kids.

What You Do

Create game boards with colored card stock or construction paper. Use a black marker to decorate the borders of one white sheet with a snake and "snake food." The hungry snake eats spiders, worms, birds, frogs, and flies, but feel free to vary your snake's food according to what's available. You may use a computer-generated border, as the designer has done here, or Halloween stickers to create your design. Leave a space (designated by a black dot) in between each piece of food. Once you are happy with the design, photocopy it onto additional sheets of paper.

• • • • •

The object of this game is to see who can feed the hungry snake all of the food on the game board first. To start the game, give each player a candy marker. If you want to use the same board for all the players, you will need to use a colored marker to indicate where each player's snake is on the board. If each player has a card, it is not necessary.

• • • • •

Players roll die to determine who will go first. The first person to roll "snake eyes" (the two on the die) begins the game. Players continue to roll the die and move clockwise around the board. The player whose snake eats all the food first (and gets all the way around to the snake's mouth) is the winner. If a player lands on the alligator (or any other beast of your choosing), the player must return to start.

What You Need

• Squares of card stock or construction paper in Halloween colors
• Permanent black marker or computer-generated border
• Colored pencils (optional)
• Candy for game markers (candy corn or candy pumpkins)
• Die

designer: **BARBARA STEPP**

designer: **SANDIE BISHOP**

Halloween Ghoul Pin

A marbled polymer clay leaf in autumnal colors is a striking backdrop
for an easy-to-make molded face; make the face look as terrifying
or good-natured as you wish.

What You Need

- Polymer clay, ¼ block each green, gold, brown, and red
- Commercially made press mold or materials to make press mold (small figurine, soft brush, talcum powder, and a piece of scrap polymer clay)
- Leaf
- Craft knife
- Pin back
- Hot-glue gun

What You Do

This designer used a commercially made press mold, but you can make your own. All you need is a small figurine or doll, a soft brush, talcum powder, and some scrap polymer clay. Shape the clay into a pad slightly larger than the face or figurine, brush some talcum powder lightly onto the doll's face and the pad of clay, then gently press the powder onto the face. Remove the pad of clay and gently reshape, if necessary. Bake the face mold using the time and temperature recommended by the polymer clay manufacturer.

. . . .

Blend together the four colors of polymer clay (green, gold, brown, and red) by repeatedly pressing, stretching, and folding the pieces of clay together. Make sure the colors remain separate from each other, forming ribbons of color.

. . . .

If you are using a commercially made press mold, follow the manufacturer's instructions and make a face mold out of the marbled polymer clay you have created. After the face is removed, use your fingers to shape additional ghoulish facial features, such as wrinkles or dimples.

. . . .

If you are using a mold you created (see above), brush the inside of the mold with talcum powder, roll a ball of marbled clay large enough to fill the cavity and some to spare. Elongate one end of the clay slightly, and press the elongated end into the mold. Use a craft knife to trim the back and sides of face, then ease the soft clay face out of the mold with your fingers. (Chilling clay for about half an hour will help with hard-to-release molds.) Smooth any irregular edges with your fingers and shape face as needed. Bake the face according to manufacturer's instructions.

. . . .

Work the remainder of the marbled polymer clay into a ⅛-inch (.3-cm) thickness on a clean work surface, making sure the piece of clay is wide enough to accommodate the size of the leaf. Press a leaf into the clay hard enough to leave vein imprints. Trim around shape of leaf with a craft knife, then lift leaf carefully off of work surface.

. . . .

Press molded face onto leaf close to the bottom of the leaf, and carefully shape the leaf around the face as desired. Bake according to manufacturer's instructions. When piece is completely cool, hot-glue pin back to the back of clay leaf.

No Thanks,
Yallery Brown

LATE ONE SUNDAY NIGHT, as a young English boy named Jim crossed the west field on his way back to the farm, a wailing cry arose from the tall, green grass. He thought it sounded like a baby who had lost its mother, and now lay weeping alone under the stars in the warm July darkness. The boy stopped to listen for a moment, cocking his head to see where the cry was coming from. He would help the poor child, if he could only find it!

He followed the sound through the darkness as best he could, and crawled through the brambles at the edge of the field on hands and knees, pricking his fingers on thorns as he felt around in the dark weeds. Finally, his knees stained and his fingers stinging with pricks, the boy sighed a long, tired sigh. He would have to give up. Just as he was about to rise to his feet and turn back toward the farm, he heard the noise again right beside him. This time, the boy seemed to make out more than the familiar whimpering sound—he thought he could hear words.

"Oh, the stone! The awful, huge stone! Oh, help, I can hardly breathe under the stone!" a strange little voice whined. This was not a baby at all, he realized, for even boys of sixteen knew babies couldn't talk.

He crouched back down on his hands and knees and moved a few feet further in the tall grasses. Suddenly, grasping in the darkness with his right hand, he felt a cold, hard stone. He scuttled forward to the stone, and, feeling it with both hands, made it out to be about the size of a watermelon. He could then see the stone in the moonlight. It was large and flat and weather-beaten in its place under the weeds.

"Oh, oh, the stone! The awful, huge stone!" came the sobbing little voice again, and the boy knew he must do something. However, he had also heard that it could be very bad luck to meddle with the evil Little People, or the tiny creatures who lived among the stones of the earth. His own people would often turn their roads in a new direction to avoid overturning the sacred stones of the Little People.

But this Little Person did not want to be under his stone, the boy thought, so it must be okay to move it. With that, he grabbed the large stone with both hands and, letting out a loud grunt, wrenched it out of the earth. There, in the black dirt of the hole beneath it, lay a tiny Little Person, staring up at him with two gleaming black eyes still wet with his tears.

Though the tiny creature was no bigger than a baby, he looked very old. He had long, knotted hair and a long, matted beard that covered his entire body, all the way down to his knees. His hair was a bright yellow, like spun gold, and looked as silky as a maiden's wedding gown; but his face and his skin were a dark brown, almost the color of dirt. He was as wrinkly as a plum, the boy noticed, and decided the creature must be older than 100.

For a moment, the boy and the Little Person sat stunned in the moonlight, surprised and amazed at the sight of each other, until finally the Little Person hopped to his feet and scampered out of his hole. "Jim, my boy, you've done a fine good deed," said the Little Man to the young boy. The boy was quite taken aback, for he wondered how the tiny old wrinkled creature that had been living under the stone could possibly know his name. Was it a goblin of some sort?

"Nope, nope, nope, not me, not me!" sang out the tiny, yellow-haired man. "No goblins here!"

This time, the boy was glad he was already on his knees, for he was shaking so hard he would have surely fallen down, had he been standing up. How had the creature known what he was thinking?

"You'd be better off keepin' all your questions to yourself, my boy! Just be sure I'm a good friend of yours, the best you'll ever have!" the creature sang out with a wide grin and a sparkle in his black, black eyes.

The frightened boy took a deep breath and gathered all his strength and courage. He had to find out who this Little Person was. "I have just one more question," he said to the sprightly creature dancing gaily on his toes in the weeds beside him. "Wha—What's your name?"

"My name, eh?" the Little Man piped in his squeaky voice. "Call me Yallery—Yallery Brown, that'll be me name!"

The boy thought that a rather queer name, but, upon studying his new friend, realized that the tiny man was indeed very yellow and very brown.

"What shall I do fer ya, Jimmy?" Yallery Brown asked, suddenly springing to the boy's knee and staring him straight in the face. "Anything ya like, I can do it. Shall I find you a wife? Spin you a thousand dollars? Cook you a feast fit for a king?"

Jim thought a moment. None of these offers sounded as good as the one he had in mind. He was a somewhat lazy young boy, and would much rather spend his days lolling about in the haystack or under the apple tree than shoveling feed in the stables or minding the horses. What he would really like, he knew, was someone to help him do his work.

"Work!" sang out Yallery Brown. Jim had again forgotten Yallery could read his mind. "That's it then. I'll give ya a helpin' hand in yer work, cause you've jest given me more help than you'll ever know by rollin' over that there stone. It's a fine deed you've done, my boy, a fine deed indeed."

"Why, thank you, thank you," Jim began, excited at the thought of getting a rest from his daily chores.

At hearing his words, however, Yallery Brown's eyebrows drew up into two angry arches, his black eyes got dark as storm clouds, and his lips bent into a sour frown. "No!" Yallery Brown screamed, in a ferocious version of his high-pitched little voice. "No thanks! No, no, no!" he yelled, stamping his tiny bare foot on the earth. "The one thing you must never, ever do is *thank* me," he warned Jim. "For that, you will be sorry." And then, Yallery Brown plucked a dandelion puff from the ground and blew it so that the little hairs scattered everywhere. Jim shut his eyes until the dandelion hairs landed. When Jim opened his eyes, Yallery Brown was gone.

The next morning, Jim awoke before daybreak, as usual, and set out for the stables to start his chores before breakfast. But, when he got to the stables and looked about, he could hardly believe his eyes. All the work was done already! The horses had been turned out, the stables cleaned, and everything put away. There was nothing left for him to do. He picked a piece of straw from the haystack, stuck it in his mouth, and spent the day lying in the shade of the apple tree.

Day after day, this pattern continued. Each morning, Jim rose to do his work, but found all of his chores already finished. If the farmer gave him other chores to do, Yallery Brown saw to it that those were done, too, and Jim would sit idly by while the singeing irons or the pitchforks or the hoes worked away, all by themselves, without a hand to guide them.

At first, Jim thought this was a wonderful deal. All of his chores were done, even better than he had ever done them, and he got paid good money for doing nothing. But soon, instead of simply doing Jim's work well, Yallery Brown began to undo the work of the other farmhands. He filled Jim's buckets with water, but spilled the other hands' water. He sharpened Jim's tools, but blunted the others' tools. The other boys suspected Jim of causing these things, began to talk about Jim behind his back, and gave Jim mean looks when they were near him. They even threatened to tell the farmer about Jim's mischief. "This has to stop," Jim thought, "or it will be no use having someone else do my work at all."

One morning, standing in the clean stable by himself, Jim called for Yallery. "Yallery Brown, come from the meadows, I must speak to you!" Jim felt a sharp pinch on the back of his leg, and when he wheeled around with a yelp, there stood tiny Yallery Brown, as yellow and brown as ever.

"Okay, Yallery, I'll thank you to stop doing my work and to stay out of my life from here on out," Jim told Yallery in a bold voice. As soon as the words had left his mouth, the tiny man's face broke into a wicked grin, and he let out a wicked laugh as he began to dance an evil jig on the sawdust floor.

"What did I tell ya, my boy?" Yallery Brown sang out in an evil, cackling voice, still dancing round and round. "I told ya never to thank me! And now you've gone and done it! You've thanked me!"

Jim didn't realize he'd done it, but, now that he thought about it, he guessed he had thanked Yallery Brown. He wondered what horrible trouble this would bring. He stared

at the evil imp before him with fear, as Yallery Brown, still whirling in circles, began to chant:

"Work as you will,
You'll ne'er do well;
Work as you will,
You'll ne'er gain nought,
For harm and mischief and Yallery Brown
You've let out yourself from under the stone!"

Yallery Brown chanted the song twice more and then, in a whirl of golden hair, he wrapped himself up in his long yellow beard and blew away like a dandelion puff. Shaking and dizzy in his fright, Jim ran from the stable, stumbled over a fence, and headed for home, never to return to his job at the farm again.

Yallery had cursed Jim indeed. For whatever job Jim tried, he could never succeed or prosper. Eventually, he married, but all of his children died and his wife was often ill. The animals on his farm stayed sick and skinny, and his garden never grew. He remained poor and desperate until his last days, when he could only sit on the porch in his rocking chair and hear the wicked voice of Yallery Brown ringing in his deaf ears:

"Work as you will,
You'll ne'er do well;
Work as you will,
You'll ne'er gain nought,
For harm and mischief and Yallery Brown
You've let out yourself from under the stone!"

Skull and Crossbones Tote

This simple tote bag is a fresh alternative to plastic pumpkins and grocery bags, and can be constructed in short order. It works especially well with pirate costumes (see page 112).

designer: **TAMARA MILLER**

What You Need

- 2 pieces of black fabric, 12 inches (30.5 cm) square (felt or wool work well)
- ¼ yard (.2 m) white fabric
- Scrap of black fabric for the handle
- Sewing machine (optional)

What You Do

Determine which square of black fabric will be the front piece. You will need to attach the skull and crossbones to this piece before you sew the bag together. Cut out simple skull and crossbones pieces from the white fabric. Position the design on the front piece, and use a zigzag stitch in white (on a sewing machine) to secure. You may also sew the design on by hand, if desired. Create a mouth by zigzag-stitching with black thread or hand-stitching. (This designer personalized the bag with an initial on one bone.)

. . . .

Once the design is in place, position two black squares with right sides together and sew together with a ½-inch (1.5-cm) seam allowance. Turn the bag right side out. Make a handle out of a scrap piece of black fabric by cutting a piece of fabric and hemming edges, and stitch handle ends to each side of the tote.

mine's bigger than yours!

Growing pumpkins is remarkably competitive. Every year in early October, pumpkin growers around the world flock to designated sites to weigh their most promising pumpkins. Official representatives of the Great Pumpkin Commonwealth, established in 1993, call in their winning pumpkins and, if a new record is set, the lucky pumpkin is registered with *The Guinness Book of World Records*.

Sinister Twist Game

*You'll be surprised at how much fun both children and adults will have
with this Halloween take on a traditional favorite.*

design: **TAMARA MILLER**

What You Need

- Transparent shower curtain
- Patterns for Halloween motifs
- Five different colors of construction paper, 5 sheets each
- Craft glue
- Cardboard
- Construction paper for the grid, 1 sheet each of 4 different colors
- Black permanent marker
- Bendable wire
- Metal bead

What You Do

You can draw your own Halloween images or use the patterns we've provided (page 152). You will need five copies of each image. Cut around the images and glue each to the center of a piece of colored construction paper. (All five of the same image should be glued to the same color paper.) If you wish, words can be used instead of images.

• • • • • • •

Spread the shower curtain out flat and position the pieces of paper on the curtain in an even grid. One by one, apply glue to the construction paper, flip paper over (so that image is against clear plastic), then press down firmly against plastic to secure. Allow the curtain to dry for several hours before using. **NOTE:** You can also use a white tablecloth or sheet for this game, though the shower curtain makes it more durable.

• • • • • • •

To make the spinner board, cut a piece of cardboard (the size of the spinner board can vary), and use construction paper to create a four-part grid. The parts are for the left foot, right hand, right foot, and left hand. Use a black marker to mark sections. You will also need four (reduced) copies of each Halloween image for the spinner board.

Make a spinner by twisting wire together. Make a hole in the center of the cardboard, pull end of wire through to the other side, then bend end of wire to secure spinner in place. Use a metal bead to raise the wire pointer off the board; this will make spinning much easier.

• • • • • • •

This game should be played with two to six players. It is helpful to have one person who is designated to control the spinner, as it becomes difficult for players to spin for themselves. Each player rests the appropriate body part (foot or hand) on the designated image. A player is out of the game when he or she can no longer hold the position on the board.

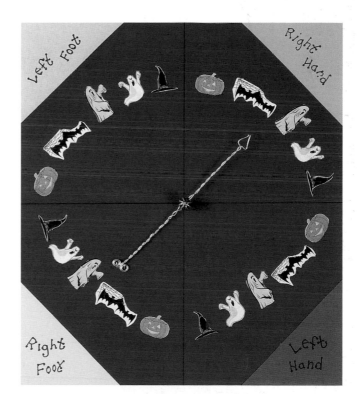

chilling body parts

Fill nonpowdered surgical gloves with water and tie the wrists together with twine, a twist-tie, or a rubberband. Position gloves on cookie sheet and place in freezer. Peel the gloves off and use ice hands for a creepy addition to Halloween punch. A plastic mask (with duct tape placed over the eye and mouth holes) makes an equally eerie ice face.

Play Clay

Making homemade play clay is a fun and easy children's project—and it makes a great party favor. The result is a wonderfully touchable substance that is nontoxic and nicely scented. Add to the amusement by allowing your guests to decorate their own place mats with permanent markers.

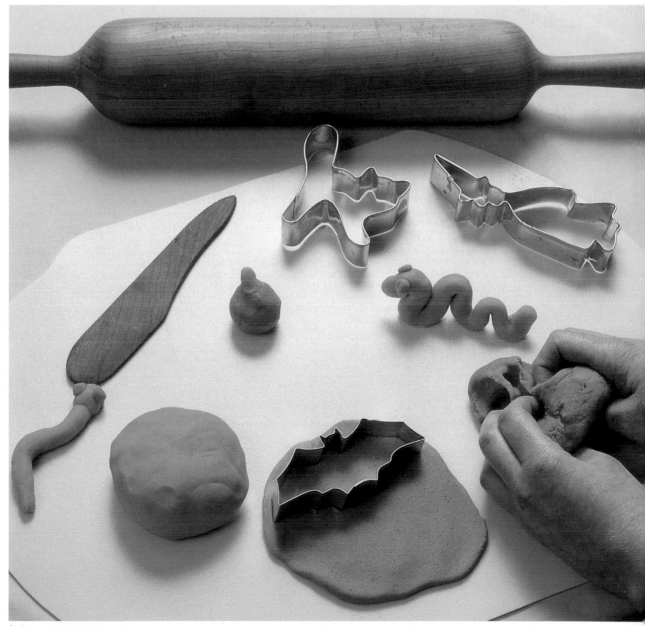

designer: **BARBARA STEPP**

What You Need

- 1 cup (125 g) all-purpose flour
- ½ cup (288 g) salt
- 2 teaspoons cream of tartar
- 1 cup (240 ml) cold water
- 1 tablespoon vegetable oil
- A few drops of food coloring
- Flavoring of your choice; pumpkin pie spice (orange clay) and peppermint oil (green clay) were used here
- Small saucepan
- Small bowl
- Wax paper
- Vinyl place mat

What You Do

Mix together the flour, salt, and cream of tartar in a small saucepan. In a separate bowl, mix water with oil. Add water mixture to dry mixture, and cook over medium heat until mixture forms a ball in the pan. Turn out onto wax paper on countertop and allow to cool for several minutes. Add food coloring and flavoring to clay as you knead it. Store in an airtight bowl or plastic bag. Keeps longer if stored in the refrigerator. **NOTE:** do not double recipe, as it does not work as well.

• • • • •

Allow children to create shapes with the play clay on a vinyl place mat. Provide cookie cutters and dull tools for making various shapes. For a Halloween party, have a contest to see who can create the best jack-o'-lantern or the scariest monster.

Paper-Mache Tarantula

Startle your houseguests with this terrifying paper-mache tarantula. A grouping of these furry spiders are a hair-raising addition to any haunted house; they are particularly frightening when positioned so that they appear to be emerging from a dark, mysterious place.

dogs and chocolate

Chocolate is toxic to dogs. Do not allow your children to share their Halloween loot with the family pet, as it can be fatal.

What You Need

- Coat hanger
- Black acrylic spray paint
- Plastic triangles
- Light bulb
- Ball of tape
- Craft glue
- Instant paper mache mix
- Scrap of artificial fur, white
- Brown shoe polish
- Plastic artificial jewels

What You Do

Cut pieces of coat hanger for the legs, use your hands to shape the pieces, then spray-paint them with black acrylic paint. Make sure you make a hook on one end of each leg, so that the leg will have mobility inside the spider. Cut pieces of plastic into triangles (plastic cups work well) for fangs/feelers. Set aside legs and fangs.

· · · · · · · ·

Use a light bulb for the back of the spider and a ball of tape for the front (or head) piece. Attach the two pieces with craft glue and allow to dry. Mix the paper mache according to the manufacturer's instructions. Cover the entire surface of the body of the spider (the light bulb and the ball of tape) with paper mache. While the paper mache is still wet (but after it has set up somewhat), insert plastic triangles and coat-hanger legs into paper mache. Allow to dry thoroughly—at least two hours.

· · · · · · · ·

Remove the plastic triangles, then spray-paint the body with black acrylic paint. Allow to dry thoroughly. Replace fangs. Glue artificial jewels (for eyes) to the spider's head, just over each fang. Cut a piece of white artificial fur to fit on body of spider. Rub brown shoe polish across top of fur to create highlights in fur. Glue fur in place.

designer: **DANE BARKER**

Contributing Designers

DIANE ARKINS is a writer and crafter who lives in Olympia Fields, Illinois. She collects vintage Halloween memorabilia in her spare time.

DANE BARKER has studied drawing and painting and is currently the office administrator for Lark Books Catalog Division. He is assisted daily by his trusty canine, Golda.

BUTCH BASSETT is a history major at the University of North Carolina at Asheville and works as a technician for a cellular phone company.

TERRY BREWER is a culinary student at Asheville-Buncombe Technical Community College. He also has a degree in art, and hopes to be a food consultant and cookbook author when he graduates. He lives in Pisgah Forest, North Carolina.

ROGER BRIGGS is a produce vendor and distributor at the Western North Carolina Farmers' Market. His painted pumpkins are in demand throughout the fall. He lives in Flagpond, Tennessee.

PAMELA BROWN is a professional candlemaker who owns and operates Mountain Lights, a candle and lighting shop in Asheville, North Carolina. In addition to her line of hand-dipped candles, she creates candleholders made from recycled products.

LISA COLBY is a jeweler whose works are featured in galleries throughout the United States and London. Originally from Detroit, she now resides in Asheville, North Carolina, with her daughter, Celeste. Lisa has a sentimental affinity for bees (thus, her costume design on page 130), which, according to folklore, are messengers from heaven.

PERRI CRUTCHER owns and operates Perri Ltd., a floral decor studio in Asheville, North Carolina. Perri specializes in creating gorgeous floral designs around found objects, and has worked with such world-renowned floral designers as Renaldo Maia (New York City), Setuo Kitono (ikibana master and tea-flower design expert), Christian Tortu (Paris), and Robert Isabel (New York City).

KELLY DAVIS is a product development specialist at a craft publisher and, thus, has her finger on the pulse of the craft world. She lives in Asheville, North Carolina, with her children, Bailey and Zachary.

SUSAN EDWARDS is a supervisor for the telemarketing department at J Crew in Asheville, North Carolina. In addition to creating unusual costumes, she sews, beads, and makes her own jewelry.

MELANIE FRANCE is a National Sales Director for Gannett News Services. She also designs, knits, and sells children's vegetable hats. She resides in Biltmore Forest, North Carolina.

BONNIE HALL is a registered nurse and nursing instructor who lives in Arden, North Carolina, with her husband, Steve. She is an avid sewer, but also spends time quilting, painting ceramics, gardening, and cooking.

ANDREA JERNIGAN is a biology major at the University of North Carolina at Asheville. She works at a local nursery and hopes to own her own herb farm when she graduates.

CHERYLE KINLEY teaches fourth grade at Catawba Springs Elementary School in Denver, North Carolina, where she is the school's technology mentor. She resides in Stanley, North Carolina.

CORKY KURZMANN is a teacher who enjoys educating children in her community through craft projects. Known for her high energy level, Corky spends her free time gardening, canning, preserving, and herbal crafting.

TAMARA MILLER is a stay-home mom and crafter who lives in Hendersonville, North Carolina, with her son, Beck, and her husband, Jeff. Her crafting interests include making Santas and Christmas stockings, as well as projects that involve her son.

CHRIS NOAH-COOPER specializes in cut-and-pierced paper lamp shades, scherenschnitte, etchings, and faux-finished frames. She is an art teacher and art therapist, and her work has appeared in *Better Homes and Gardens* magazine. She resides in Miamisburg, Ohio.

JEAN WALL PENLAND is an artist who paints and teaches in the North Carolina mountains. She has received both Pollock-Krasner and Adolph and Esther Gottlieb Foundation grants.

CATHERINE REURS, a former career banker in Europe, is an internationally recognized needlepoint and cross-stitch designer. Her work has been featured in more than 70 magazines, including *Traditional Home*, *McCalls Needlework*, and *Country Living Magazine*. *Splendid Needlepoint*, her second book, was published by Lark Books in 1997.

MERCEDES RIOS-YOUNG works in Asheville, North Carolina, as a public affairs assistant for the U.S. Forest Service. She grew up in Virginia, and surprises friends and family with her creative handmade Halloween costumes every year.

HEATHER SMITH, editorial assistant at Lark Books, has mourned the loss of her pet fish Goldie since 1983. Designing the fish tank costume (see page 124) was a way to give tribute to her lost friend. Heather grew up on the coast of Maine, where she taught environmental education. She now enjoys exploring around her new home in the mountains of western North Carolina.

BARBARA STEPP has been a kindergarten teacher in Henderson County, North Carolina, for 15 years. Barbara's kindergartners and grandchildren benefit from her creativity in sewing, designing, and crafting. She lives in Hendersonville with her husband, Bobby.

LINDA STOCKTON is a doll artist in Waynesville, North Carolina, who makes one-of-a-kind dolls. She has been a featured artist in *The Cloth Doll* magazine, and her dolls have been published in *Contemporary Doll Collector* and *Soft Dolls and Animals.*

GINGER SUMMIT is a retired teacher who lives in Los Altos Hills, California. She is an expert gourd artist and the author of *The Complete Book of Gourd Craft* (Lark, 1996). Her passion for creating with gourds is especially evident around Halloween.

TERRY TAYLOR specializes in creating art for the garden using pique-assiette, or shard art, technique. Terry is known for his willingness to try any craft—and does a fabulous job at whatever he tries. He collects, creates, and carves from his home in Asheville, North Carolina.

KIM TIBBALS-THOMPSON resides in Waynesville, North Carolina. She is a frequent contributor to craft books and enjoys drawing, sewing, gardening, herbal crafting, and broom making. By day, she is a graphic designer.

KATHLEEN TRENCHARD owns and operates Cut-It-Out, a company that designs and manufactures cut-paper products. Her work explores the possibilities of cut-paper as an art form. She lives in San Antonio, Texas.

NICOLE TUGGLE is a marketing assistant in Asheville, North Carolina. She spends her free time exploring her passion for paper and book arts; she especially favors the personal aspect of mail art.

PAMELLA WILSON is particularly in tune with costumes and face painting, since she was formerly a professional clown. In addition to these skills, Pamella is an accomplished potter and visual artist.

MELANIE WOODSON lives in Asheville, North Carolina, where she is a whiz crafter. Mosaics, polymer clay, painting, beadwork, needlepoint, knitting, metalwork, and stained glass are only a few of her many talents. When she's not creating something beautiful, she sings in a band.

Index

**LARK
BOOKS**

FOR A FREE CATALOG
of our complete line
of distinctive craft books,
write to
Lark Books
50 College Street
Asheville, NC 28801 USA
Or in the continental U.S. and Canada,
call 1-800-284-3388

website: www.larkbooks.com
e-mail: larkmail@larkbooks.com